How to Coach a Woman

In the busy-ness of being so caught up in the minutiae of life I sometimes find myself so overwhelmed I just want someone to 'offload' onto. It's not ideal if this is my poor long-suffering husband or even my best friend because there can be stuff that's simply too private or, more importantly, something that seems huge to me yet I know if I tell someone close to me they'll judge me and tell me I'm being ridiculous. Perhaps I am! I don't usually feel in need of psychotherapy or even counselling; what I need is a coach, but specifically a coach who really understands women just like me.

Lynette Allen and Meg Reid have years of experience of coaching and understanding women and have some refreshing new suggestions on how to connect with us. As they point out, a woman wouldn't go into a gents' outfitters and expect to find the perfect fitting garment, so why go to a coach who isn't expert in coaching women?

There is some great research and information in *How to Coach a Woman* together with some really fun and practical ideas. I loved the 'wheel of life' diagram and along-side it a 'wheel of strife'! How brilliant that they present what stresses the average women – perhaps your client – in an amusing way.

If you're already a life coach, or interested in becoming one, or a manager who wants to connect with the women you work with, then this book is for you. I'm none of the above but I still found it fascinating just to learn about the psychological differences between men and women, and it was comforting to know that some of my inner-most thoughts are quite universal!

Janey Lee Grace, author of *Imperfectly Natural Woman* and founder of 'The Home of Natural Alternatives' at www.janeyleegrace.com

A fantastic coaching handbook for women, *How to Coach a Woman* is a practical guide on how to work best with brilliant women.

Suzy Greaves, founder of the Big Leap Coaching Company

How to Coach a Woman is refreshingly practical, stin̶ authors have generously gifted their expertise to th̶ women and men alike!

Katherine Tulpa, CEO, Assu̶c̶.̶.̶.̶

How to Coach a Woman

How to Coach a Woman – A Practitioner's Manual

A refreshingly different guide to becoming an ethical and responsible coach

Lynette Allen and Meg Reid

Crown House Publishing Limited
www.crownhouse.co.uk
www.crownhousepublishing.com

First published by

Crown House Publishing Ltd
Crown Buildings, Bancyfelin, Carmarthen, Wales, SA33 5ND, UK
www.crownhouse.co.uk

and

Crown House Publishing Company LLC
6 Trowbridge Drive, Suite 5, Bethel, CT 06801-2858, USA
www.crownhousepublishing.com

© Lynette Allen, Meg Reid and Crown House Publishing Ltd, 2012
Extracts on pages 3–4, from *Committed* by Elizabeth Gilbert, published in the UK by Bloomsbury and in the US by Penguin Group (USA) inc., reproduced with kind permission.

The right of Lynette Allen and Meg Reid to be identified as the authors of this work has been asserted by them in accordance with the Copyright, Designs and Patents Act 1988.

First printed 2012.

All rights reserved. Except as permitted under current legislation, no part of this work may be photocopied, stored in a retrieval system, published, performed in public, adapted, broadcast, transmitted, recorded or reproduced in any form or by any means, without the prior permission of the copyright owner. Enquiries should be addressed to Crown House Publishing Limited.

British Library Cataloguing-in-Publication Data
A catalogue entry for this book is available from the British Library.

ISBN 978-184590676-4 (print)
       978-184590052-6 (mobi)
       978-184590051-9 (epub)

LCCN 2010937322

Printed and bound in the UK by
Bell & Bain Ltd, Glasgow

Crown House Publishing has no responsibility for the persistence or accuracy of URLs for external or third-party websites referred to in this publication, and does not guarantee that any content on such websites is, or will remain, accurate or appropriate.

Acknowledgements

This book is dedicated to all the colleagues, coachees and students we have ever had the pleasure of working with, coaching, teaching and mentoring. Without their input, their inspiration, their willingness to see possibility and change, this book would never have happened.

We would like to thank you all, in particular those who have contributed to parts of this book: Melody Akena, Shay Allie, Shelley Blackburn, Gabrielle Blackman-Sheppard, James Carter, Gwen Channer, Jessica Chivers, Jill Crossland, Carole Dodd, David Edwards, Sophie Eld, Tamara Furey, Paula Hart, Helen Hind, Jo Hockey, Sue Houghton, Rebecca Hourston, Audra Lamoon, Clare Lindstrand, Gordon Melvin, Dr Lillian Nejad, Sarah Oakley, Sarah Owens, Professor Stephen Palmer, Jane Price, Juliet Price, Lisa Quast, Hetty Reid, Mark Spall, Geraldine Steele, Sydney Tyler Thomas and Razwana Wahid.

Lynette Allen and Meg Reid

Foreword

In the past twenty years we have seen a rapid growth in the field of coaching services. The industry has progressed from life and personal coaching to high powered executive and leadership coaching. I can recall a decade ago criticising the lack of references in most coaching books whereas even this has improved more recently. The industry has gradually matured with professional bodies setting up coach accreditation and course recognition schemes as well as developing codes of ethics and practice.

However, when we look at the field it becomes apparent that there has been a lack of publications that focus on coaching women although there have been a couple of notable exceptions. Lynette Allen and Meg Reid have now co-authored this book, *How to Coach a Woman*, which includes various theories, coaching models and frameworks with numerous examples of the coach–coachee dialogue which brings alive the process of coaching. The authors share with us their perspective on coaching women and highlight their observations.

The authors illustrate the TGROW coaching framework; the acronym stands for **T**opic, **G**oal, **R**eality, **O**ptions and **W**ill/**W**hen/**W**hy. TGROW sets the scene for the coaching journey that both the coachee and coach travel as they work together, with the coach facilitating the process in order for the coachee to achieve their realistic goals. Within this framework the coachee develops the well-known SMART goals. However, the authors also introduce the reader to their own coaching acronym, FEMALE, which focuses on coaching for women. FEMALE stands for **F**ocused (she is focused on being able to take positive steps towards that one goal alone); **E**mpowered (she is taking ownership of the goal, which is to do with her and no one else); **M**easured (she is able to find a scale of measurement that fits her style in order to understand how close she is to attaining her goal); **A** stands for **A**ligned to her ethics and beliefs (she is able to articulate how the goal runs alongside those ethics and beliefs that she holds dear); **L**inked to her **E**motionally (that she has bought into her goal emotionally and has made a link between the practical solution oriented steps and the reasons *why* she would take those steps).

Lynette Allen and Meg Reid are to be congratulated for sharing with us their experience of coaching women and highlighting useful models and frameworks to enhance the coaching process.

Professor Stephen Palmer
Director of the Centre for Coaching, London

Contents

Note to the Reader

In this book, we refer to our experiences of coaching both genders and of training women and men to become coaches. We quote relevant scientific research where appropriate but we are not suggesting that either gender is superior or that anyone, female or male, is condemned by their genes or their life experiences to certain behaviours.

Where we quote evidence of brain difference, we acknowledge that the scientific world is divided as to the significance of neurological discrepancies between the sexes, and that some researchers argue that quoting what they call 'neurosexism' places obstacles in the way of the development of both genders.

In her book *Delusions of Gender*, Cordelia Fine (2011) argues that any variations between the brains of men and women are soft not hard wired, so the resulting behaviour patterns and abilities are flexible and changeable.

Lise Eliot, Associate Professor at Chicago Medical School, argues that we don't inherit intellectual differences, but they are the result of what we expect boys and girls to be and to become.

To whatever degree we are influenced by biology, in our experience we are all affected by society's understanding of what it means to be female or male.

Introduction

When ... someone listens to you, when another person has the time to sit opposite you, take in and concentrate on what you're saying without agenda or judgement. When someone has no advice to give and won't make any up. When someone doesn't presume they know what's best for you, won't publicise your affairs around the office or gossip about you to your friends. When the person listening to you believes you can juggle what you do, rearrange what you have, reprioritise what you need and change your mind – if you want to. When someone doesn't mind that you're confused, won't be emotionally scarred by seeing you cross, disappointed, upset or irritated. When for that hour, it's absolutely, entirely, completely and totally OK just to be you.

You can't tell us there isn't a woman alive who would love an hour in that place! Well, if you are a professional life coach, a business or executive coach or use your coaching skills at work, as a manager, the skills you have provide that place; coaching is needed and valued by its female coachees because it provides that place. The coaching skills you have, and want to build on, will be of more use to a woman than any invention, gadget or technological progress could ever be. This book will show you how to communicate with women using a coaching approach.

It will also teach you how to talk to women about coaching and what to expect from your female coachees. It will give you tips, techniques and proven coaching models to take your coachees through so that you get to the heart of the matter and deal with issues swiftly. In short, it will not only describe all the skills you need to coach successfully but will teach you the primary differences between coaching a woman and coaching a man.

Are there really differences we hear you ask? Surely coaching is coaching, no matter what gender your coachee is? Well, it may surprise you to learn that there are huge differences between coaching men and women. Coaching, as you will find out, can be quite different when you focus on one gender and become an expert in that field.

For centuries we've been trying to work out the core differences between men and women. Sociologists and psychologists have argued about whether the differences between the genders thrown up by their research are caused by biology or by society and the way we are brought up – in other words, the nature or nurture debate. Some assert that how we behave has evolved from the work we do: that the ancestral hunter/gatherer roles and the more modern division of work into paid work outside the home and unpaid work in the home has resulted in gender differences in personality and behaviour (Archer and Lloyd, 2002).

The neurobiological differences between the genders may have an effect on male and female behaviour. Some studies for instance, suggest that women have a higher percentage of grey matter in comparison to men, and that men have a higher percentage of white matter and cerebrospinal fluid. These physical differences may affect the way men and women think. Late twentieth-century studies have shown the effects of hormones on the human brain and our behaviour.

Other researchers look to the way we are brought up to explain the often puzzling or irritating mismatches in the ways that men and women think and communicate. One could argue that the way we are socialised as children has a significant effect on the way we communicate as adults, that we take that in-built initial socialisation into our adult lives – that it's ingrained in us, so it's no surprise that it affects the way we communicate as adults. (For more information on this particular issue, we found some very interesting research at www.iteslj.org)

Research presented in John Archer and Barbara Lloyd's *Sex and Gender* (2002) suggests that, even today, boys and girls are brought up differently. They refer to studies which show that the traditions of giving boys cars and girls dolls continues. They cite 'numerous North American studies [in which] there was clear indication that both parents encouraged "gender typed" activities'. Even the way their bedrooms are decorated will be very different for a brother and sister (cited in Archer and Lloyd, 2002: 62–63). Parents we've interviewed who had actively encouraged their sons in the first 36 months of their lives to watch less violent, traditionally 'girl' oriented cartoons soon found that their sons started denouncing them (and the fluffy toys they'd been given) as 'for girls'. They seemed entirely uninterested in the miniature ironing boards and vacuum cleaners they had been specifically given to play with – seeking out instead anything vaguely resembling a stick, which they then used to throw at each other, fight with and express themselves in competitive war type activities. They were just playing, of course, but they seem to have picked up on the boy/girl expectations of society even at this tender age.

As adults, it seems that there is no getting away from the traditional roles of women as the main caretakers in society. In her book *Committed*, Elizabeth Gilbert seeks to understand the value of marriage and the effect it has on women. She says:

> I do not entirely understand why the women to whom I am related give over so much of themselves to the care of others, or why I've inherited such a big dose of that impulse myself – the impulse to always mend and tend, to weave elaborate nets of care for others, even sometimes to my own detriment. Is such behaviour learned? Inherited? Expected? Biology predetermined? Conventional wisdom gives us only two explanations for this female tendency towards self-sacrifice, and neither satisfies me. We are either told that women are genetically hardwired to be caretakers, or we are told that women have been duped by an unjustly patriarchal world into *believing* that they're generally hardwired to be caretakers. These two opposing views mean that we are always either glorifying or pathologizing women's selflessness. Women who give up everything for others are seen as either paragons or suckers, saints or fools. (Gilbert, 2010: 172)

Later on, Gilbert also highlights how women are traditionally the ones who adapt and move emotionally and physically around their families to willingly accommodate and put first everyone else's whims and expectations. She says:

> [Women have] it has always seemed to me, a sort of talent for changing form, enabling them to dissolve and then flow around the needs of their partners, or the needs of their children, or the needs of mere quotidian reality. They adjust, adapt, glide, accept. They are mighty in their malleability, almost to the point of a superhuman power. I grew up watching a mother who became with every new day whatever that day required of her. She produced gills when she needed gills, grew wings when the gills became obsolete, manifested ferocious speed when speed was required, and demonstrated epic patience in more subtle circumstances. My father had none of that elasticity. He was

> a man, an engineer, fixed and stead. He was always the same. He was
> *Dad*. He was the rock in the stream. We all moved around him, but my
> mother most of all. She was mercury, the tide. (Gilbert, 2010: 183)

It seems that for all our twenty-first century challenging of traditional gender roles at work and in the home, the basic principle remains that women and men, despite our common humanity, experience life differently. That difference has been the stuff of literature, music, politics and the workplace for generations. That difference will naturally inform and influence the way you coach your female coachees.

In Jane Austen's *Persuasion* the then current male/female social roles are described in this way:

> The Mr. Musgroves had their game to guard, and to destroy, their
> horses, dogs, and newspapers to engage them; and the females were
> fully occupied in all the other common subjects of housekeeping,
> neighbours, dress, dancing, and music.

In the famous musical *My Fair Lady*, when a frustrated Professor Higgins can't understand why Eliza has run away, he sings in 'A Hymn to Him':

> Women are irrational, that's all there is to that! ...
> They're nothing but exasperating, irritating, vacillating, calculating,
> Agitating, maddening, infuriating hags! ...
> Why can't a woman be more like a man?

And much more recently, in David Lynch's cult 1990's TV series *Twin Peaks*, Agent Cooper remarks: 'In the grand design women were drawn from a different set of blueprints' (quoted in Archer and Lloyd, 2002: 2).

How can we interpret these studies from a coaching perspective? Regardless of where your loyalties lie in the nature/nurture debate, wouldn't it be refreshing to acknowledge that men and women do in fact behave differently? Instead of trying to suppress those differences and pretending they don't exist, it would be infinitely more advantageous at this stage in our development to recognise those differences and work with them within the coaching framework. Within the coaching fraternity there is simply a need for coaches who are expert in understanding the detail of those differences, so they can become super-effective at supporting their female coachees when traditional 'male' perspectives don't work for them. Women, after all, have been mistresses of adaption and change where required over the centuries; now it is time for the coaching system to rejuvenate and breathe fresh life into its processes, inspiring the women of tomorrow by supporting and recognising the needs of women today.

A woman wouldn't expect to walk into a man's clothes shop and find a perfect fit. She wouldn't expect to walk into a man's shoe shop and find a perfect fit. So why on earth would a woman expect to go to a coach who isn't an expert in coaching women and find her perfect fit? Masculinity and femininity are complex issues and most people will have what we label 'masculine' and 'feminine' aspects to their personality and behaviour. But we would like you to benefit from our experiences in coaching women so that you can hone your skills to work with your female coachees (whether you're a manager coaching at work or a professional coach) more successfully.

This book will give insights into how women think and therefore how a coach can be trained to use his or her approaches, terminology, questions and rapport building skills to find that perfect fit. Notice that we said 'his or her' approaches. To our minds, it is entirely appropriate for a man to become an expert in coaching women, just as it would be for a female coach to coach male clientele. This book is about helping you get a perfect 'fit' with how a woman thinks – the types of issues that run through her mind, the speed at which her mind works, how a woman communicates and much more. What it is *not* about is diminishing the importance of men and how men think.

Coaching a man and coaching a woman is simply different – very different. This shows up clearly in the linguistic styles of the sexes at home, work, in meetings, on social occasions and in personal, casual and formal contacts. According to Deborah Tannen, 'communication isn't as simple as saying what you mean. How you say what you mean is crucial, … using language is a learned behaviour: how we talk and listen are deeply influenced by cultural expectations. Women and men are like people who have grown up in two subcultures' (1995: 138). Women and men tend to have different ways of saying what they mean, which is why we feel this book is so important.

The TGROW model (which we cover in Chapter 3) is traditionally taught as a one-stop shop for the perfect coaching scenario – to coach anyone on any topic. However, we will go one step further and show you how to sculpt this model, and your thinking, to fit your female coachee perfectly.

We will do this by concentrating on our six key principles to coaching a woman. They are:

Key Principle Number 1
Women want to feel their relationship with their coach is unique and different from the coach's relationship with other coachees

Anson Dorrance, from the University of North Carolina, in his article 'Coaching Women: Going against the Instincts of My Gender', says:

> Although I was young, when I was first asked to coach the University of North Carolina (UNC) men's soccer team in 1974, I was prepared. Being male, and a devoted athlete and scrappy soccer player myself, I understood training men. The shock came in 1979, when I was asked to coach the women. The feminist literature at the time was telling me there were no differences between men and women; however, I have spent nearly my entire career discovering, and appreciating, those differences ... Women relate through an interconnected web of personal connections, as opposed to a more traditional male hierarchal style. To that end, what is critical in coaching women is that all players on the team have to feel like they have a personal connection with their coach, and it has to be unique.

Although Dorrance is talking about coaching football here, the same goes for coaching women throughout their lives. Each of your female coachees need to develop a unique relationship with you. One whiff of thinking she's 'just another coachee' or that you are working to a formula which is the same for all your coachees and she will be off, in search of a coach who really 'gets her'. Women foster their own unique relationships all the time. They have one friend who 'listens', one friend who 'gives advice', one who does 'sympathy', one who does 'straight talk', and they value each and every one of those friends – just as they will value their coach and the unique relationship they build with him or her. Men just don't seem to make that distinction between their buddies. We will teach you how to make that unique connection by getting to know the 'world' women live in – understanding how their children and partners fit into their lives, understanding what their responsibilities are, what is important to them and what their priorities are.

Key Principle Number 2
Women learn best through discussion and have highly developed verbal skills

In cognitive tests and tasks which highlight sex differences, women obtain higher scores in verbal fluency. In coaching sessions, the fact that your female coachee will do most of the talking is paramount; it is how she learns about herself and how she solves her problems.

We know that women love talking and so coaching would appear to be a brilliant fit, but if the coach misses the key principle that, for women, talking is more than just streaming words and careless nattering, they will be missing a vital female preference and the coaching relationship just won't be as satisfying to either coach or coachee.

In our experience, we have found that our female coachees use talking to find things out about themselves – things they didn't realise were true until the moment the words left their lips. Women use talking to connect to others and to solve problems. Talking gives women access, in a unique way, to the information they hold in their unconscious minds.

Key Principle Number 3
Women have the ability to fix several problems at the same time, even when they are only talking to you about one issue

Women are renowned for their ability to multitask in everyday situations and we've noticed this when our female coachees are problem solving in a coaching session. Some research has suggested that while men use only one hemisphere of the brain to perform a function, women will use both (Jäncke and Steinmetz, 1994). In *Brain-sex*, about the biology of gender and the biological differences between men and women, Anne Moir and David Jessel (1998) suggest that women generally distribute processing across diverse regions of the brain. Male brains (testosterone modified versions of the female brain) are notably more 'compartmentalized' and 'focused' in their processing.

This is the science behind the popular language of women having a natural aptitude for 'multitasking', and men seeming to generally adopt 'single minded' behavioural strategies. Discussing theories behind both men and women's ability to multitask, Karen Pine, Professor of Developmental Psychology at the University of Hertfordshire said that in experiments where men and women worked on a series of simple tasks at the same time, such as searching for a key while doing easy maths problems, the women significantly outperformed the men, concluding from this that women are better able to multitask than men.

This may be why your female coachee might be telling you one story but her mind will already be fixing another problem simultaneously. It is why it is important to let her stream vocally – without judging that streaming as inconsequential chatter – and it is also why letting silence happen in the right place at the right time will be crucial to her.

A woman's mind, when she is being coached, will flit all over the place and you need to be ready for that. An expert in coaching a woman will understand when is the right place to give your female coachee time to fix solutions in her mind that she won't even have told you about. Because that is what women do: their minds race at 100 miles an hour even when they are silent or apparently daydreaming. One of our coachees described to us how her husband had noticed that she had been deep in thought when she was driving them to town. They were sitting in comfortable silence: her husband was enjoying being driven for a change and our coachee was consciously aware of where she was driving and what she was doing. She began, however, to tap the steering wheel with her thumb – an action she hadn't noticed but her husband had. After looking at her for a few seconds, he smiled and said 'What are you thinking about?' She explained that she had just driven past a block of industrial units and wondered what it would be like to run her business from there and whether she would walk to work. She wondered how much the business rates would be and what the business community in that block was like, whether it was welcoming and engaging. All of those thoughts had been running through her mind as she had driven the short length of the block and been concentrating on dealing with heavy traffic and a roundabout. She had been thinking on multilevels. Your coachee will do that while being coached by you.

Key Principle Number 4
Women are emotionally literate and so are willing to acknowledge, explore and express emotions

In our experience, corroborated by research highlighting that 'women show greater emotional sensitivity and responsiveness than men' (Grossman and Wood, 1993), women are far more likely to feel comfortable talking about and expressing emotion during a coaching session. In fact Kuebli, Butler and Fivush (1995) have shown that girls' propensity to talk about emotion shows up early in childhood.

Women seem to have an enhanced awareness of 'emotionally relevant details, visual cues, verbal nuances, and hidden meanings', writes Robert Nadeau, the author of *S/He Brain: Science, Sexual Politics, and the Myths of Feminism* (1996). In an essay on this subject in *The World & I* (1 November 1997), a personal attributes questionnaire lists female-valued attributes including, 'does not hide emotions', 'aware of other's feelings' and 'expresses tender feelings' (quoted in Archer and Lloyd, 2002: 23).

Of course, there are many men who aren't afraid to show their emotions, as Alexander McCall Smith says in his novel *Corduroy Mansions*: 'We all weep, the only difference being that men often suppress their tears.' It is your female coachee though who, in our experience, is most likely to talk openly about how she feels and even to cry during the session.

Sociologist Deborah Tannen, author of *You Just Don't Understand: Women and Men in Conversation* (1995) studied the differences between how men and women use conversation. It would seem that for males, conversation is the way they negotiate their status in a group and keep people from pushing them around, whereas women use conversation to negotiate closeness and intimacy.

When your female coachee has established this closeness and trust with you as her coach, you will be able to react differently from her friends. Crying on a best friend's shoulder is a comfort, but to be in a place where you feel safe enough to talk openly about what you feel, what you want and how to make the changes you need, is a real gift. We will show you how to create that space for your coachees.

Key Principle Number 5
Women are able to use visualisation very effectively

According to research referred to in *Psychology* (Carlson and Buskist, 1996: 471–472) women have been found to be consistently superior to men in tests involving visual recognition. Ecuyer-Dab and Roberts (2004) cite evidence to show that when giving map directions women are more likely than men to give landmarks – women picture the route as though they are seeing it – whereas men describe the distance or the direction to take. Understanding how to work with a highly visual woman will give you greater depth and insight into coaching her.

Our female coachees often use visual metaphors to explain what they are thinking about. For example, one coachee described her confusion about her work–life balance as 'having my thoughts in a tumble drier'; another visualised her life choices as boats going in different directions. Using visualisation techniques to picture the results of doing something differently is immensely motivational for a woman. We will teach you how to harness this visual ability to help your coachee see her future success.

Key Principle Number 6
Women are more self-critical

When involved in tests relating to spatial awareness, more women than men reported feeling confused but the researchers attributed this to women believing that they are less capable and competent than they really are.

A major study conducted by researchers at the University of Wales Institute (UWIC), Cardiff (Sanders, Sander and Mercer, 2009), which explored self-esteem in 112 psychology undergraduates, found that, compared with their female contemporaries, male respondents had higher self esteem, expected higher marks in exams and anticipated performing better than their fellow students. However, across the UK university sector female students continue to achieve more 'good' degrees (firsts and 2:1) than male students.

This self doubt seems to start in childhood. Teachers tell us that boys are quick to answer questions in class without worrying if they are right or wrong; girls on the other hand don't answer unless they are sure they are right and, even then, phrase their answers as a question. In her keynote speech to the American Library Association annual convention in 1994, Susan Herring proposed that 'women and men have different characteristic online styles'. The female style is characterised by 'apologizing, expressing doubt, asking questions, and contributing ideas in the form of suggestions' as well as being supportive and appreciative (Herring, 1994: 3–4).

We find that our female coachees, even those who hold senior corporate positions, often question whether they are doing well enough. As women climb those corporate ladders, there are few, if any, blueprints for how a woman should juggle her life when she's there. We are the first generation of women to be reaching these dizzy heights. Who does a woman turn to when she's unsure how to be a woman in a powerful role, when how she 'thinks' she is meant to behave and how she instinctively 'feels' it is right to behave conflict? Coaches fill that role in a way that a woman's friends cannot.

A survey conducted by Aspire Companies in 2008 (www.aspirecompanies.com) entitled 'Women Who Make It Work: The Secrets of Success for Female Leaders', found that 'women leaders who want to achieve the greatest success need to have some kind of process in place to enable them to set (and continue resetting) a clear inspiring vision'. Coaching provides this space. On the contrary, her friends will only try to make her feel better, and they will do that by arguing that she is just as good as her associates, they will point out how competent she has been, they will highlight her successes, put down others even, in an attempt to make their friend see for herself how wonderful she is. That approach won't work though. Instead, a coach takes her concerns seriously, validates them by being interested in the details and then asks how she would like to change. Stepping stones towards that change can then be laid for the coachee to walk on with confidence because their foundations were taken seriously.

A coach who doesn't understand how these six key principles fit into a coaching relationship with a woman simply won't be doing her justice.

Women have choices in today's world but of course, 'choice' brings with it uncertainty and confusion. This is where the coach comes in – where your training, your acute listening skills and your heightened sense of a woman's values and abilities can play a direct part in her future. Coaching can mean the difference between your coachee sinking, procrastinating and missing opportunities, or feeling like she is standing her ground, directing the elements of her life with ease and taking control long term.

In essence, coaching is a structured conversation – one that won't be allowed to go round in circles or degrade into gossip. There is a purpose to it and a desired end result. In this book we will teach you how to structure your session, how to avoid the pitfalls of coachees who can't seem to get past a certain issue and how to gently move a coachee to a solution that feels right for them. Skilled and experienced coaches will be able to use that structure flexibly to help shift a coachee from confusion to clarity, and their coachee won't be able to see the seams. It will feel like a rewarding conversation, where they got to say their bit, explain the complexities of their situation and feel that their opinion mattered.

A woman needs space in which to think clearly about what she wants, without being told what to do or criticised for what she thinks. She needs somewhere to escape to for an hour – somewhere to plan, mull over and think – away from the demands of her family and work commitments. Women use coaching because they want to be inspired, held to account and motivated. Your future coachees are just waiting to be able to say to someone, 'I'm not sure how to do this,' without worrying they will lose face. Coaching offers the time to enable women to make important decisions differently, when the 'for' and 'against' arguments confuse them and when commitments are piled high on their plates. It was no surprise that Allison Pearson's book *I Don't Know How She Does It* (2002) was a bestseller. Most of us smiled in recognition as the heroine tries desperately to juggle her roles of mother, wife and professional with to-do lists which feature preparing a major presentation for the Board, beside a note to make her daughter's costume for the school nativity play. You can see why the importance for a woman to stop and draw breath is paramount.

Our coachees tell us:

> **'I'm looking for someone who is like-minded to me.'**

> **'I want someone who is going to help me understand what is actually going on. Not lecture me, but help me find the answers I know are there but are frustratingly not forthcoming!'**

> **'I want someone who is reassuring, on my side, encouraging/ energising and who makes me really think. Normally I'm looking for a sense of direction with an issue. I want to feel I've got somewhere I wouldn't have got by myself.'**

> **'I want a much better understanding of why I've got to a decision or chosen a certain path.'**

This is what your future coachees are looking for and we will teach you just how to give it to them. We will be covering every aspect of what it takes to coach a woman – from making her feel listened to, helping her to understand the options available to her and exploring options she may never have thought of before. We will be explaining the importance of knowing where your coachee is going and ensuring she gets there. We will be honing your questioning skills, developing your understanding of positive thought and explaining how values, self belief, self esteem and confidence are linked to a woman's life. By the end of this book, you will feel more prepared than you thought possible to cope with any situation your female coachee might present to you, and will be inspired by what your skills could achieve.

1 Barriers, Myths and Laying Down the Ground Rules of Coaching

Unfortunately, it has been all too easy for people to call themselves a coach without being qualified and without understanding how a coach should support his or her coachees. As a result, there are still a few myths surrounding the industry which we feel it is important to point out – not only so that you feel well prepared to dispel them if and when you come across them, but also so you understand how to approach your female coachees and move around the industry ethically and responsibly.

If you are already a coach, you will know the time and effort required to understand what coaching is and the training, application and skill needed to become a coach of excellence. Your qualification means that you've taken this seriously, that you've been taught and trained how to get the very best out of your coachees. For those of you who are yet to qualify, you are about to enter a very worthwhile profession. It is our job as coaches to educate the public about coaching, what its boundaries are and the level of skill a coach must acquire to be able to do his or her job properly.

We've heard all sorts of myths throughout our coaching careers, from 'So, you're going to solve all my problems then!', 'You must have a pretty perfect life' and 'Coaching is money for old rope' to 'Surely coaching is the last resort?', closely followed by 'So, you're going to tell me where I'm going wrong' and, the best one of all, 'You're half my age, you've no life experience, how can you tell me how to live my life?'

Sadly, it is women who have made some of these comments. In our experience, it can be easier for a man to view coaching as a practical tool to shift obstacles out of the way and move forward. It is often seen simply as a business technique – and for many men emotion isn't linked to the reasons they might use that method. On the other hand, it can be difficult for a woman to hire a coach if she believes that you only turn to one when you can no longer deal with your problems yourself. Myths like this aren't true or helpful if we are to promote coaching as an excellent professional and self development tool.

This chapter puts those myths to bed and gives you some ethical guidelines to pass on to your coachees when they ask about coaching.

The myths

'So, you're going to solve all my problems then!'

The aim of a coach is to be able to support her/his coachees as they make positive changes to their lives. We are experts in being able to bring the best out of people and help them access solutions that will work well in their own lives. These solutions will probably not work in the same way or to the same extent in anyone else's life. Remember, coaching isn't one size fits all; it is about unique solutions to unique lives. We are not experts in other people's lives, which means the coach will not be diagnosing, sorting out problems or directing the coachee in any way. The coachee is still likely to encounter problems or difficulties after their coaching session, but hopefully the strategies they choose to put in place as a result of those coaching sessions (after their perspective of their capabilities or indeed their perceived limitations were challenged) will mean that they are much more likely to negotiate problems with greater ease and confidence in the future.

Melody Akena, Managing Director of Clara House Residential Home, is just one example of how coaching continues long after formal sessions are completed. She says:

> Coaching has given me many invaluable skills and one of them is the ability to plan out a project clearly and avoid my common failing of over-commitment. Before I was coached, everything (and I mean everything) seemed insurmountable and unobtainable; not even my most positive attitude could see me around some of the demands of my job as a care manager and a business owner. In one session that all changed. It's a bit like a 'being with the end in mind' approach. I literally think of what I want to achieve, write it down in all the glorious details and bring pictures in if I need to. I then work backwards, looking at what I would need to apply to achieve the goal, project or overcome the situation. I have four headings – costs, people, time and resources – with my own subheadings underneath which can vary. I do this so often I can now start the process in my head, having

identified the situation. This helps me to ensure that I stay on track in business, and more importantly, my time is managed as I can stay confidently within time frames, whether I can commit to situations or not, and everyone is happy.

Melody makes several important points here: that this skill was learnt during her very first coaching session, that her mind is flexible enough to work backwards and forwards, that she uses visual images to make her outcome seem real and that she can do this in her mind, even before she starts the process formally. All of these points highlight the six key principles outlined above, so she is a perfect example of how coaching a woman works in practice when she is working with a coach who is very aware of the way a woman's mind works.

'You must have a pretty perfect life'

Coaches are normal human beings! We sometimes make mistakes, make the wrong decisions, say the wrong thing occasionally and yes, like everyone else, may find that we'd like to change some things in our lives too. Coaches do not have a book of life's answers, but they do have a heightened awareness of their communication skills and knowledge of some very effective exercises (a number are included on the accompanying CD) that might help them access unique solutions they can use in their own life. That's not perfection; it's awareness. Coaches understand the value of being coached and will often have regular sessions themselves to make sure that, as life moves forward, they are going in the right direction for them. So it might seem like they have everything on track, but they will be working to achieve that every day, just like their coachees.

'Coaching is money for old rope'

You are unlikely to take on a new coachee who genuinely believes this statement. Coaching doesn't have a 'product' to show for its time and effort. Changes that are made to a coachee's life are often powerful yet subtle. Ask a coachee who was coached six months ago what difference it made to their lives and you are likely to get a long list of everything they've changed or achieved. Ask them five minutes after their session and it may not be so immediately apparent.

Therefore, it is sometimes difficult to see what a coaching coachee comes out of their session with. As a result, some coaches offer feedback reports for their coachees detailing what they spoke about, the areas they covered, what the main issues identified were and what they decided to do differently as a result of their session (a sample form appears on the accompanying CD). Fabulous light bulb moments where coachees get a revelation during their sessions *do* happen, of course, but certainly not every time. Change happens but lasting change occurs over a time period.

We spoke to former coachee Shelley Blackburn, Managing Director of Essex School of Beauty (www.esbeauty.co.uk). She used her sessions to focus her mind and to speak to her coach as a sounding board when talking ideas through with staff and family wasn't appropriate. She says:

> Usually I came to the coaching sessions with set issues, ideas or topics to talk through. When I wasn't sure where to take something or how to deal with a situation, I found it very helpful to talk to someone confidentially who didn't judge my professional capability on my confusion about a certain issue. I'm actually a very quick worker and it doesn't take long for my ideas to get formulated; by the next coaching session I'd usually have ticked off everything I'd spoken about previously and then some. When I spoke about a bigger issue though (getting another business off the ground, Indulgence at Home), it took much longer to bring my ideas to fruition and so the immediate effects of the coaching session I had on that topic are only just beginning to be felt a year on.

> That session sparked a lot more research about the new business. I wrote down everything we discussed and the many, many options that were open to me and have spent the past year researching them, honing them and being able to implement the actual tasks that were a real fit for my new business. This was a much bigger task for me and it wasn't until, over time, I was able to reassess all the options that came out of that session for realistic value, that I was able to move forwards. I'm there now and plans are taking shape to launch it, exactly as I want.

We also have an example of the perceived financial value of coaching from some research done by one of our students. The students aren't allowed to charge for their practice sessions while in training but one of them decided to ask his volunteer coachees what they would have been happy to pay for the coaching session they'd just had with him. The answers ranged from £50 to £200 for one hour of coaching from someone who was still in training. There is no doubt that coaching makes a significant impact on people's lives.

'Surely coaching is the last resort?'

Take a look around you at the office, have a think about the women in your life and how they live their lives. Can you think of someone in control, who is a strong role model, who seems to succeed easily, who has an air of confidence about her? We wouldn't be surprised to hear that she has employed a coach to achieve that level of balance. Coaching is rarely a last resort: strong, intelligent women who want to succeed will constantly be looking for ways to improve and strategies to streamline their commitments. They will be interested in self development; they will understand the power of having a sounding board and of being listened to. It is often women who are of that ilk who seek coaching. It should never be seen as a last resort and you don't have to be a quivering wreck for coaching to be a valuable part of your life. Those women who saw coaching as a last resort, but took the plunge and hired a coach, will tell you they wished they had done it years before!

'So, you're going to tell me where I'm going wrong'

All recognised, professional coaches will have a code of ethics (there is an example on the accompanying CD) to follow by their accrediting body, which will state that we are not allowed to perform diagnoses. One person's wrong turning is another person's saving grace. It is not up to us to say who is wrong and who is right. In actual fact, when coachees start explaining how their lives run, when they reveal how their relationships with those closest to them work or when they describe the ins and outs of a particular work issue, any 'mistakes' they are making often become very clear to them. That is the beauty of being coached by a complete stranger: when you begin to articulate the issues obvious patterns of behaviour start to emerge. If you think your behaviour, decisions or viewpoint should be different, you will work with that – but you will never catch a reputable coach telling you how to do any of those things.

'You're half my age, you've no life experience – how can you tell me how to live my life?'

We find that children are sometimes excellent coaches because of their tendency to ask 'why' all the time:

MUM: Get your coat on, I promised I'd take Mrs Walker to her dentist appointment.

CHILD: Why?

MUM: Because I promised.

CHILD: Why?

MUM: Because I was being nice.

CHILD: Why?

MUM: Because I always try to be nice.

CHILD: Why?

MUM: Because I was brought up that way.

CHILD: Why?

MUM: Because it's important to put others first.

In practice, the word 'why' will be used only with caution by a qualified coach (we will go into more detail about this later in the book), but in this case, the child identified that her mother was brought up to believe that 'it's important to put others first' in five simple words!

Here is a perfect example of a how a child, with no life experience, can offer a line of questioning that cuts right to the heart of why her mother offered to take a neighbour to the dentist. When we have to explain how things run and why we do things, we often see more clearly where our habits and beliefs lie – which can produce momentous light bulb moments for any woman. A good, effective coach can be a 5-year-old, a teenager or a grandmother. Age and life experience aren't the issue, asking genuine questions that probe are; and it is 5-year-olds who often know how to do that without even being taught!

Laying down the ground rules

OK, so now on to the ground rules of coaching. Set these out at an early stage when a coachee calls you to talk about how you work and you will set the stage for a professional, ethical and responsible coaching relationship.

When a potential coachee phones to talk about coaching or e-mails us for more information, we are unlikely to launch straight into our fee structure and where to meet up. What we are after initially is an understanding of who is on the other end of the phone, what they might want coaching for and whether we are the right coach for them. 'Chemistry' between coach and coachee is vital and if you can establish that on the phone or in an e-mail in the first instance, you are more likely to build a relationship based on trust and respect. We might well ask her some of these questions:

> **'What would you like to get from coaching?'**
>
> **'What is it that attracts you to coaching?'**
>
> **'What was it about my website/flyer that drew you to call me?'**

These questions will also establish how much of an understanding your potential coachee already has about the coaching process and how you work. After all, she may have been coached many times before or she may have literally stumbled across your website on the internet and felt compelled to pick up the phone. You will notice that all of the above questions are open questions. We have a whole chapter dedicated to honing your questioning skills (see Chapter 4), but for now, it is enough to know that open questions – questions that start with 'how' and 'what', for instance – naturally promote chit-chat, which will help you get to know your coachee-to-be. That first conversation will help both of you determine whether you might enjoy talking to each other and working together.

Once you've established that coaching is right for the coachee and that you could well be the right coach for them, the next step would be to explain what to expect. You should aim to cover the following points:

- **You won't be giving her advice.** Of course she may have contacted you exactly because she wants someone to tell her what to do. Maybe she has already spoken to friends who have passed on their ideas and solutions. Maybe she has already done what other people think she should do. Maybe a rebellious voice inside her has said, 'I'm *not* going to do what they're telling me.' But no one else is living her life; no one else knows her true feelings. As her coach you will help her to find her own answers but won't make her decisions for her. One of our students, Clare Lindstrand, saw the power of never giving advice during her training:

> Personal experience tells me how important and valuable being non-directive is in providing an open and positive space where coachees can grow and respond to themselves differently, finding solutions that are right for them. In a session with the owner of a small business, (I'll call her) Penelope described having tried many times to improve her organisational skills to make her business more efficient. Penelope had attended courses, read books and paid consultants to change the way she worked. After just one coaching session addressing the topic and developing her own personal methodologies, Penelope described being 'more committed than ever' and 'feeling more energised and focused'. Six months later, I was delighted to hear in another session that her new strategy was 'working wonders' and that the tools she herself had developed were 'miles ahead of anything the textbooks had ever taught her'.

- ***You are committed to your coachee being true to themselves and that you won't be attached to any particular outcome from their sessions.*** So if your coachee is a working mum of three and tells you she would like to sail solo around Europe, then you will work with that dream and your coaching will help your coachee to put strategies in place towards making it a reality. Unlike family or friends, we won't be tutting that she should be concentrating on her children's dreams and not her own, for instance. If your coachee tells you that she'd like a better relationship with her boss, it is not up to us to determine whether that would be a good or a bad thing; if that is what she wants to work towards, then her coach will support her in that aim.

- ***You have been trained to coach using a proven technique, yet you will work with it flexibly and will be able to mould that tool to fit her preferences and personality – exactly what a woman needs.*** Remember Key Principle 1 – women do not want a one-size-fits-all method to their coaching; they are after an individual relationship with you and a personalised approach. Therefore, even though the standard coaching model we will show you in this book will be used every time, your approach to each coachee will be unique.

- **Everything you talk about will be confidential.** You won't be reporting to her boss or gossiping about her to anyone else, and any records you keep of your meetings will be kept safely in accordance with the Data Protection Act.

- **It isn't your job to judge her.** Remember Key Principle 6 – women are already self critical and will feel as though people are judging their decisions in everyday life. She will need to know that your coaching approach is different. As women, we often feel a pressure to show how well we are doing. Mums compare their children's reading ages or how many words their toddler can say. At work we want our line manager to think we are confident and capable. We worry about other people's judgements about us, which often means we are hesitant to ask questions or admit that we need help. Coaching is a conversation where a woman can be herself without worrying about playing a role or hiding her fears and insecurities.

- **You will use this time to let your coachee know how you work in terms of admin.** How she pays, whether you will talk on the phone or face to face, when the session will happen and any cancellation policy you employ will all need to be laid out clearly and upfront. You may wish to use your own simple terms and conditions to send to a coachee with your information or confirmation letter (sample templates can found on the accompanying CD) if this would work for you. Make these points clear now to save confusion later.

- **Explain how many sessions a coachee may need and how often.** Some coaches prefer to book sessions in groups of four or six, some prefer to work one session at a time. We've known coachees to take just one session and it has been enough to make huge differences in their lives. For others, it is regular contact and a commitment of time that works best for them. In practice, sessions should be near enough together that the coachee doesn't lose focus, but far apart enough that they have time to reflect on the changes they've made and take any promised action. Weekly, fortnightly or monthly tends to work well. It is important that your coachee knows they can stop the coaching process at any time and pick it up again in the future if they wish. As for how many sessions, work with your coachee; she will know what benefit she is getting and when to stop. Remember

Key Principle 3 – your female coachee can fix lots of problems at the same time – so to say that for six issues she will need six sessions could be wildly inaccurate. Your coachee's mind is quick, fast and multilayered so telling her how many sessions she will need won't be your best approach.

- **Cover the issue of what contact you offer between sessions.** Most coaches offer their coachees a proportion of e-mail contact between sessions – how much is completely up to you. Again, when you think about how you want your practice to run, consider the kind of business and lifestyle you want, whether you have children or elderly parents to look after – these factors will all determine the amount of time you'd like to give to each coachee. There is no right or wrong way of doing this, other than to carry out what you state you do. Take a look at the terms and conditions on the accompanying CD as this might help you set out your business as you'd like to continue.

- **Point out that your coachee needs to have an idea of what they'd like to talk to you about before their session.** However, it is not important for you to know what that is in advance; in fact, we'd go as far as to say it can be a handicap to know what your coachee wants to talk about before you meet them (more about this later). Your coachee needs to understand that coaching is a process in which they will take the lead role; it is not something 'to be done to them'. Therefore it is helpful if the coachee comes prepared with an area of their life they'd like to talk through, along with an idea of what they'd like to gain from the session itself. In short, your coachee must be prepared to change something or want something in her life to change for coaching to be really effective. It might be that your coachee doesn't know, that she just has a feeling of unrest or dissatisfaction. She might be asking herself questions such as 'Is this all there is?' It is absolutely fine to take on a coaching coachee who is thinking that, just as long as you are both aware that the process and structure of the sessions is such that a suitable topic will need to be found and a specific goal worked on. You can use the first part of the session to let your coachee talk about her feelings of unrest. Remember Key Principle 2 – discussion, discussion, discussion. Your female coachee has highly developed verbal skills and so, to her, chit-chat isn't just mindless talk. Chit-chat means organising topics, kicking out options, bringing new options to the fore, gaining understanding and clarity. Talk is important; letting your coachee talk is what will give her direction, so don't insist she has that clarity before you meet her.

- ***You might be asked what the difference is between coaching, mentoring and counselling.*** These three disciplines are what we call 'talking therapies' and use listening, questioning and summarising skills. We trained Sue Houghton, already a highly experienced counsellor, to be a coach and so she is well placed to define the differences between counselling and coaching. She says:

> Both counselling and coaching are processes many are familiar with, but sometimes it is not clear how different they actually are. Both are sources of psychological support and ways of facilitating personal change. There are various counselling orientations and many people are familiar with psychoanalytic, humanistic, person-centred and more latterly cognitive behavioural therapy (CBT). Coaching shares many features with humanistic forms of counselling, in that it is collaborative in nature – meaning that the coach and coachee work together towards a solution. The coach does not profess to be the expert on the coachee, but rather helps him/her find their own resolution to a problem; they are co-workers.

> Like CBT, coaching is a systemic process which is solution focused and results orientated. It works with core beliefs, perceptions and assumptions that are blocking the individual. These result from life experience and interjections from others. But coaching does not seek to *change* these, for it believes change can be effected without the need to understand, identify casual factors or re-experience earlier trauma. This is closer to CBT and other solutions focused therapy than some of the other orientations which have a different theoretical underpinning. Both involve ethical practice, with competence, clear boundaries and regular supervision informing the work. Empathy and positive regard for the coachee and their process is fundamental to both practices. For many there are fewer taboos associated with coaching than counselling, particularly if one is accessing help within a work environment.

Be very clear with your coachee that you are not a counsellor (unless you've been qualified in that area and even if you have, you'd need to be even clearer about which discipline your coachee is asking for). In short, the difference is this:

- Coaching enables the able, is goal driven, future and action orientated and non-directive.
- Mentoring is focused on developing by example or advice and is led by someone more experienced who shares his or her knowledge.
- Counselling/therapy is focused on feelings, understanding or healing the past, enquires into childhood, family and personal relationships.

- *A coach, even a qualified and experienced coach, must be aware of the boundaries of their discipline.* We've already mentioned that coaching enables the able. Therefore, there are certain topics that coaches are not qualified to deal with and issues that need more specialised care and help than a coach can provide. These include:

  - anyone with alcohol or drug dependency
  - someone currently experiencing severe depression or mental illness
  - someone with an active eating disorder
  - someone suffering with traumatic stress
  - topics surrounding sexual abuse
  - coachees engaging in illegal activities

Taking the time to make sure both you and your new coachee are on the same wavelength will make for a strong working relationship, based on trust, confidentiality and honesty.

2 Coaching a Woman's Many Faces

At this point, you might be wondering about the range of topics a woman might present with. We will cover many possible topics and scenarios in this book, but there are an unlimited number of issues and concerns that future coachees might come to you with. Although it is impossible to prepare you for all of them, we know that if you trust your commitment to the coaching process and to being a responsible and ethical coach, you will have the confidence to coach your coachees on whatever issues or problems they bring to your door.

In this chapter, we will give you an idea of the areas of micro-niching within the 'coaching women' sector that you may like to consider. This is by no means an exhaustive list and you will see some crossover of issues, but it will give you an idea of where you might see yourself coaching. You might identify with one or two of these areas more than others and you might also have some background knowledge that would give you the confidence to start your coaching career in that area. If you have been trained to be an authentic and responsible coach, you will be able to coach in any area, regardless of your experience in that sphere. For students, however, starting with a niche in which they have experience can bring them self assurance, and often coachees will look for a coach with a background similar to their own for similar reassurance in your ability.

We've identified ten popular female niches, together with real coachee examples, that will give you a flavour of this field.

1 Female employees/junior to middle management

If you've ever been an employee or made the move from worker to management, you will understand some of the issues that surround women in these areas. We've highlighted a few below from real life examples but it is also interesting to note one of the conclusions of a survey conducted by Aspire Companies in 2008, which found that 'balancing work with home and navigating male-dominated work environments' were the top two barriers facing women. Typically women in these roles are facing the following issues:

- How can I stop myself from working until it is time for the last bus home?

- My boss's behaviour is unpredictable and I don't know how to approach him/her.

- I feel bullied by a colleague and need to understand how to assert my authority.

- I'm split between leaving on time for my family commitments and staying late to be part of the team.

- I work with someone who is trying to undermine me and I need strategies to deal with this.

- I've got some big egos in my team and don't know how to get them to work together.

- My assistant isn't pulling her weight and is very moody – how do I get the best out of her?

- I'm so exhausted after looking after my family and working, my needs get forgotten.

- How do I get noticed and make an impact in my organisation?

- I'm not satisfied at work any more and don't know what to do.

Eleanor came for coaching because she had been promoted to manage the team she used to be part of. She needed to work out how to make the transition smoothly so that the staff who had previously seen her as an equal would now accept her in her new role as their manager. She also wanted to make a good impression on those senior to her. As the previous manager had been forced to resign unexpectedly the staff were unsettled. She felt it was vital that she made a good impression from the beginning and establish how she wanted to work. At the same time she had to take on a large volume of work she wasn't familiar with. She felt she couldn't discuss her worries with anyone in the organisation without seeming weak or even risking losing her new status. Nor could she find a suitable internal mentor or role model for her new role. This is a common problem in our experience. Collins and Scott (1978) state that everyone who 'makes it' has a mentor, but women at work often find it difficult to achieve this kind of support. In their 2008 survey 'Women Who Make It

Work: The Secrets of Success for Female Leaders', Aspire Companies found that '2 in 5 of survey respondents couldn't think of a single inspirational female leader' and that finding a mentor was 'least likely to be considered a strength' for a woman by employers. There is no surprise then that coaching is filling that need.

Coaching gave Eleanor a space to reflect on her specific areas of concern – how to relate to her team/senior managers – and also let her voice her insecurities without fearing any repercussions. Spending an hour away from the office gave her the chance to think and plan.

She had six sessions with her coach, sometimes working on how to develop a specific project or how to prepare for an important meeting, sometimes talking through the best ways to inspire and support her team. Because of the nature of the coaching space she was also able to see how well she was already managing, which left her feeling far more confident in her ability to carry out her new role.

2 Female business owners/entrepreneurs

Typically women in these roles are facing the following issues:

- How can I grow my company?

- I'd like more confidence to network at business events.

- I want more coachees and have so many ideas, I often don't know which one to work on first and so end up doing nothing.

- I'm at the stage where I need to take on help, but the transition to employing people is very daunting.

- I work in a family business and need a strategy to be able to see them without talking about work all the time.

- I want to be taken seriously when pitching to predominantly male teams.

- I'm working late into the night and waking up checking e-mails – I need a long term strategy.

Amanda sought coaching because her business was growing more quickly than she had anticipated. The extra workload and demand was pulling her enthusiasm down and she wasn't at all sure how to go about taking on staff or interviewing for people to help her. Her coach did not give her the answers, but their conversations involved understanding how to increase her confidence in running a larger organisation, where to find the legal answers she required and how to research her business further. After six weeks, she put together two job descriptions for assistants, started advertising the vacancies and understood the financial and legal implications of employing her first two full time employees. Taking on these staff freed up Amanda's time to be able to continue growing her company, her confidence increased and the two staff she took on were a success.

3 Women in senior management and the corporate world

Women in senior management will of course have some of the same issues as business owners and entrepreneurs but in our experience it is their personal life that has a tendency to suffer. The Aspire Companies (2008) survey again backs this up: they highlighted that 68% of female CEOs say they are 'sacrificing their personal life' for their work. Other issues facing women in this field are:

- I'm overwhelmed by working in a multinational, multi-time zone company.

- My team don't pull together – how do I help them?

- I feel I'm being intimidated into bringing business into my company by using my colleagues' 'male' approach. My way is different, how can I demonstrate my value?

- My working relationship with my assistant has completely broken down.

- Someone in my team has come back from maternity leave and is being disruptive.

- I have a nanny to take care of my children but she's undermining me at home. How can I get my authority back? I would never let this happen in the workplace.

- I earn a major salary but have always wanted to work for myself – is this the time to jump ship?

- I need to increase my profile at work and I'm not sure how to do this ethically but strategically.

- I want a board position and I'm not being noticed – how do I put myself forward?

- I love my job but I seem to see my children less and less. It doesn't feel right any more and I feel torn.

We spoke to Audra Lamoon, author and owner of Livewire Performance (www. livewireperformance.com), about her coaching practice. She said:

> Being a woman in business is incredibly powerful and when I get to work closely with other women in the business world it's exhilarating. Women in senior positions network extremely well: there are no egos to placate and women are happier to give freely of their time and information. So it's always been a joy to navigate my way around this world. What happens in this industry is that when women have something to give, they give back to the women who've helped them before. What's more, women will pass on information about how you've helped them to other professionals they respect – it comes from women wanting to take care of others and preferring to work in a win-win world, rather than a competitive business society where one person's win means someone else's failure.

Audra coached a businesswoman struggling in a large corporate. She desperately wanted to start her own business but was frightened of leaving a very large salary. Over the weeks their sessions focused on facing her fears head on and asking questions around what she thought the worst case scenario would be and how she would deal with that, if it arose. Just when her coachee decided to start the business, she was made redundant. The timing could not have been more perfect. When others around her were in shock and had no idea what they would do, Audra's coachee felt prepared, confident and able to start her plans. Coaching had prepared her so well that she was able to see her redundancy as a positive opportunity to move forwards.

4 Women and relationships

Typically women are facing the following issues:

- My boyfriend needs me to be needy.

- My husband and I aren't getting on any more and I don't know how to move past our issues.

- My son has married and I don't get on with his wife; it's affecting our relationship and my confidence.

- I look after my elderly parents, which I love doing, but I'm worried our relationship is suffering.

- My partner and I don't live together and it's making life very disjointed. How can I streamline our routine?

- My mother depends on me so much, I feel I don't have space to organise my own life.

- I'd love my husband to spend more time with my family but we just argue when we talk about it.

- I've been single for a long time and have lost my confidence when it comes to dating.

- I work with my husband but we always talk about work – I need to understand how to get our personal relationship back on track.

- I earn more than my partner and it seems to be a constant thorn in our sides – I'd like to move past this now.

- None of my boyfriends ever seem to live up to my expectations – should I settle for nice?

One of the UK Coaching Partnership's qualified coaches Shay Allie is now a relationship coach (www.shayallie.com). She says:

> The best thing about being a relationship coach is that people really trust you with very intimate issues, often issues they're scared to admit to themselves even and so to be able to coach in this area is an incredible gift. Because of its sensitive nature, I find it has the biggest rewards and the biggest results. A human's most basic fear is that they're not going to be loved, I believe it's the most powerful area you can help a woman with. When love is missing, it can impact on all the other areas of your life too from your work, your weight, the hobbies

you choose, your creativity, so coaching in this area gives me a lot of satisfaction and my coachees the life they want.

One of Shay's coachees was a woman in her mid-thirties who hadn't had a boyfriend for eight years. She was a professional woman who worked long hours and was completely confident in her work but felt she lacked confidence when approaching the opposite sex. Her sessions focused on everything from what went through her mind when she saw a man she liked, to how she used her body language and eye contact. The sessions focused on what she wanted from her life long term and how she pictured herself with a partner in the future. Shay's coachee had coaching over a six month period and at the point where she was feeling much happier with herself and her confidence as a single woman, she met someone new and fell in love.

5 Women and health

Typically women are facing the following issues:

- I don't have the energy I used to and I'm not sure how to get it back.

- I'm worried my health issues are affecting my work – I need a coping strategy.

- I'm very healthy, but I want a baby later in life and want to feel fitter. How can I fit exercise into my already packed schedule?

- I've put on weight recently but I seem to have lost motivation in how to lose it.

- I feel completely stressed and don't get a buzz out of life any more.

- I'm too big to be the person I was before and I don't recognise myself any more.

- My life is out of balance and I need to get some stability.

- I haven't got time to take care of my own well-being because I'm so busy looking after everyone else but it's impacting on my energy levels.

- I'd like to learn to relax – I'm always running around and I feel tired and worn out.

- I seem to give all my energy to everyone else and find it hard to say no to people.

We asked Sarah Oakley, founder of Coaching for Health (www.coachingforhealth. co.uk), about what it is like to coach in this niche. She said:

> I love my job. I think that one of the greatest gifts that I can give a woman is space. Space to breathe and become. As a coach you are different to a friend. You listen deeply, I mean you *really* listen with pure intention, and therefore the progress made together is authentic and fantastic!

One of Sarah's coachees was a woman in her late thirties – she felt out of balance, overweight, constantly tired and stressed. Sarah reports that her coachee came to her thinking that her biggest single challenge was losing weight but in fact, through the coaching, it turned out that her goal was to love her body and make herself feel healthy again so that she could be the person she'd been hiding away from. Sarah worked with her coachee to find ways to become comfortable in her skin. Sarah reported that the greatest change came from the meditation Sarah facilitated into the coaching sessions, and her coachee making time in her week to learn yoga. With this 'me time' and meditation came a healthier mindset and healthier life choices.

6 Women of a certain age

Typically women are facing the following issues:

- My adult children are living at home – I want to move and downsize but my children won't fly the nest!

- Now I'm 50 I'm wondering what life is all about.

- I've lost my identity and sense of purpose.

- I'm going through the hurdle of a divorce and I'm not coping well.

- I'm facing illness and want to be able to deal with it positively.

- I'm caring for ageing parents and feeling stressed.

- I'm near retirement but feel there is still more I want to do with my life.

- I expected a different midlife to the one I'm faced with.

Jill Crossland (www.jbcrossland.com) is a coach for women of a certain age. She says:

> The best thing that I can say about women who are at the 'mid' point of their life is that they are ready for coaching. They ask questions, disagree at times, explore new ideas and are comfortable in being silent while collecting their thoughts. They are the ideal coachee: fully present and engaged. These women come to a session ready to do the hard work.

One of Jill's coachees sailed through turning 40; she was at the top of her game at work and looking forward to retirement, travel and time with family. Then at 44 things started to change; she became depressed, quick tempered and went from being self assured to indecisive and hesitant. Subsequent coaching revealed that she needed some time away to reflect and think. The coachee was fortunate in that she could take a sabbatical from work. Following this she realised that she was tired of her corporate job, in spite of the income. She wanted to start her own business but was unsure of her qualifications. She detailed her next step which was to find a financial planner to map out a strategy so that she had both savings and a separate fund to start the business. Her husband was supportive in terms of taking over the bills during this transition period. She went on to ascertain what business knowledge she had picked up over the years, then examined the areas where she needed training or professional advice. She also created a support team who could help her get the business up and running without going over budget. Jill continues to meet with her coachee intermittently to make sure that she is on track both personally and professionally.

7 Empty nesters

When teenagers and grown up children finally fly the nest, parents can find it incredibly hard to adapt. Suddenly parents have the opportunity to relate to each other once more, the house is quiet; how does a mum grow into that new space? Does she even want to?

For women dealing with such a major change, coaching is a precious time to take stock – to work out what it means to be 'myself' not 'mum'.

Typically women in this situation are facing the following issues:

- My child is getting ready for university and I'd like to know how to prepare myself for her leaving home.

- My daughter only seems to get in touch when she wants something – how can I create a more balanced relationship with her?

- My son isn't settling into university very well and needs a lot of phone calls. How can I support him while dealing with my own issues of missing him so much?

- I'm not sure who I am any more. I'm so used to being a mum, taxi, cook, cleaner and so on that without children to care for and run around after, I feel lost.

- My husband and I aren't getting along as well as I'd hoped now our children have left home – how can I connect again?

- My youngest has moved out and I'm living alone for the first time in thirty years. I hate coming home to an empty house.

- Long university holidays and short terms mean that we no sooner get used to our daughter's absence that we have to readjust to her coming home again – it is very unsettling.

Jill came to coaching about six months after her youngest left to share a flat with a friend. She had almost been looking forward to what she had seen as a new start in life once she had more time to concentrate on herself. She had a career she liked, some close friends and a wide range of interests. She was very surprised to find that, once she had time to see her friends and go to events that interested her, she seemed to lose motivation. She described herself as being very indecisive – unable to decide what to do with her spare time. She started projects then abandoned them. She accepted invitations then cancelled them. She described herself as trying to navigate her way around a new country without a map.

Jill used her coaching sessions to regain a sense of direction. Her first priority was to work out what she really cared about and wanted for this period of her life. She realised that some of the projects she was trying to summon up enthusiasm for were in fact old out-dated dreams which were no longer appropriate; her life had moved on. Other projects she mentioned were things that she felt other people expected her to be interested in, when in truth she actually resented being involved with them.

Once Jill knew what mattered deeply to her she was able to use her coaching sessions to work out, in detail, how to bring the things she wanted into her life. She was able to be more decisive because she was clearer about her goals.

8 Busy mums

Typically women in this role are facing the following issues:

- I've lost my identity – I'm not sure who I am any more.

- I'm uncomfortable with times when I don't have arrangements.

- I feel guilty because just being a 'mum' isn't enough to stimulate me.

- I gave up my job to be a full time mum but I'm not happy.

- I've used to run a whole department and yet, now, my 2-year-old is testing my patience, why aren't I coping?

- My teenagers no longer talk to me – I don't know what is going on in their lives any more. How can I reconnect?

- My partner thinks being at home with the children all day is easy – how can I make him realise what a responsibility it really is?

- Everyone else seems to cope so well, the other mums at the school gate look good and always seem to take part in school events. I'd like to be that organised.

- I'm not very creative and I'm finding it so difficult to help make things for their school projects or create fancy dress outfits – I don't want to let them down.

- I want to go back to work but I don't think I'll get the support I need at home.

Helen Hind, another UK Coaching Partnership graduate, is a mums' coach. She says:

> I love being a mums' coach. It gives me such a sense of fulfilment. The changes that can happen through coaching, even in the first session, can make a remarkable difference to struggling mums. Part of this I believe is just being listened to, really heard, without the conversation being stopped to be given yet more advice or deal with a difficult child. I enjoy watching my mums grow in confidence with every

session. Although it's the coachee who finds their own answers, being the one to support them is a privilege. It's not always easy to talk about motherhood and to admit if it's not 'picture perfect'.

Jayne knew exactly what she wanted to achieve when she came to coaching. A single mother working irregular shifts she wanted a social life for herself and a more established pre- and post-school routine for her children. She had already found out about some social groups in her village and knew how she would like to organise life for herself and her children. She even came to coaching with a list of what she needed to put in place. Somehow though she just didn't ever put it into practice. Jayne asked her coach if she could e-mail her several times between sessions just to report on what she had done. She said she didn't need a reply – it was enough just to know that someone was holding her accountable. Within two days Jayne had found childcare so that she could go to one of the social groups and she had invited friends round for dinner. Soon after she was able to report that she had established a regular bedtime for the children and got them involved with preparing meals which they loved.

For Jayne, taking her life seriously enough to pay for coaching was the commitment she needed to start doing things differently. Being able to tell someone in confidence what wasn't working for her and then being able to report her successes for a few weeks was just the help she needed.

9 Women in retirement

Typically women in this situation are facing the following issues:

- I'd like to go down to a three day week until I retire next year but that affects my pension.

- Now might be a good time to start the company I've always wanted – is it too late?

- I'm so excited about leaving work and have a list of things I want to do, but I feel overwhelmed with how I'll fit it all in.

- I want to keep fit in my retirement and keep my brain active – how do I do that?

- I retire next month but I haven't got any family nearby. My friends are all at work and I'm scared I'll be lonely.

- There's so much I want to do when I retire but I think my mother-in-law will expect me to do a lot more for her so I won't have any time.

- I'm dreading retirement and having to spend all day with my husband.

- I'm really worried about having enough money to have a good quality of life when I retire.

- I hate not having structure in my day and I won't have that from work any more.

Margaret wasn't looking forward to retirement. She had planned to retire at 60 and that is what she did, but in the months leading up to it she got more and more anxious about the prospect of waking up with a whole day to fill. She had always loved her work and had filled her time with meaningful activities, so although her head was telling her that she could still do the same, her heart sank at the thought of the long awaited last day. She came for coaching to 'help her heart match her head'. Margaret had three coaching sessions during which time she researched opportunities that would keep her busy and, in her searches, came across a charity that matched her personal values. After several conversations with them she is now planning to get involved with the organisation as part of her retirement plan. Margaret now recognises exactly why her heart was sinking and has a strategy that fills her with enthusiasm.

10 Mums – returners to work after having children

Typically these women are facing the following issues:

- I don't feel confident that I'll be up to speed with changes that have happened in the industry while I've been away.

- I'm worried about the effect on the children when I go back to work.

- I'm concerned about being taken seriously by my colleagues now I'm a mum.

- I'm confused about which childcare options would work best.

- I don't know if I can cope with commuting, working full time and being a mum.

- My husband is starting to sound a little sarcastic about the housework not being done at home and I feel guilty at enjoying being at work so much.

- I don't know how going back to work will affect my relationship.

Petra took five years off work with her two small children. When the oldest one went back to school and the youngest one started nursery, she was able to rearrange her home life so she could pick up her career once more. In just five years though her industry had changed so much. After a few days of researching her old network and talking to those still working in her industry, her confidence about rejoining them hit a low. Petra's coaching sessions focused on the gap she identified between her current skill set and technical knowledge and the career she had previously been very good at. Her main three topics to be coached on were confidence, technical ability and networking. Petra had six sessions in total and by the end had everything in place to confidently mix in her industry. She has used all of her strategies to find a company she wants to work for and a place within it.

Where could you coach?

Do any of these niches fit the way you would like to work? Does your background seem a good match to any particular area? Maybe this has fired off your creativity and now you've thought of an area you'd like to specialise in that you hadn't thought of before?

Do remember that in all of these cases the coaches were 'coaching' their coachees – they were not experts or mentors in these fields. Instead, they used the TGROW model to tease answers from their coachees and they used every ounce of their listening and questioning skills and empathy in coaching their coachees to success, and that's what we will demonstrate to you throughout this book.

Ultimately, if you are a sound coach, your background really has no bearing on where you choose to specialise in the future. Shay for instance, was a barrister before she trained to become a relationship coach, Audra was a hostess on a hovercraft, Helen was an insurance clerk; even we had very different backgrounds before turning coaching into our careers – Meg ran a theatre company and Lynette was a singer and dancer. Whatever your story, whatever your background or reasons for being drawn to this sector, this is an opportunity for you to be inspired and see the possibility for change in yourself and others.

3 TGROW

Suppose you had a formula that worked like magic whatever scenario your coachee arrived with? What if you had something you could hang onto as a coach, even if it seemed that your session with your coachee wasn't going anywhere or you felt confused and at a loss about what to say or ask next?

Sometimes it can feel (in the words of one of our previous students, Gordon Melvin) as if you are 'going off into the wilderness' with your coachee, hoping desperately to find a pathway out of it with them. Well, the TGROW model is that pathway. It works beautifully whether your coachee arrives knowing exactly what she wants to achieve, or whether she is stuck in a rut, hardly knowing why she has booked an appointment with you in the first place. The TGROW model is the model you will work with throughout your coaching career.

A little background on the TGROW model

If you are new to coaching and have not yet had the pleasure of being introduced to TGROW, the acronym stands for **T**opic, **G**oal, **R**eality, **O**ptions and **W**ill/**W**hen/**W**hy.

It is an extremely versatile model that will work with any topic, whether it is something practical like time management or something emotional such as wanting to feel more confident.

Your coachee has come to you because she wants to change something, she wants to come to a conclusion about something or gain clarity over something – in short, she wants her life to be different. Coaching her with the support of the TGROW model will mean that you will facilitate the coachee's movement to make the changes she wants.

The only case in which this model won't work is if your coachee doesn't really want to move forward; if, in fact, she is using coaching to prove that she is the victim of her circumstances and that she can't change anything in her life. Sometimes people are so caught up in the destructive blows life has dealt them that these negative events become a comfort blanket – something to hold on to for security. These coachees may be very reticent to let them go.

Even if you are an experienced coach, don't be tempted to skip this chapter. Each time we teach the TGROW model, we learn something new about either it or us, which improves or adds another layer to the way we coach as individuals. There is always another level of learning to be discovered. We feel it is a bit like watching a film with a complex storyline over and over again; each time you watch the film you notice another line of dialogue or giveaway look that you missed the first time. The TGROW model is no different.

It is very important to understand how to keep your coachee focused on the aim of their coaching session while also remaining 'in the moment' with them; rest assured that this will all come with practice and navigating TGROW professionally. There are times when even experienced coaches will wonder where the session is taking them – coachees can skip back and forth from topic to topic or go round in circles or feel completely stuck – but trust TGROW and it will keep you both on track.

There is no doubt in our minds – it has been proven time after time by coaches the world over – that this system works. Stick with it. Be flexible with it. Weave confidently through it. It will work.

Before the first session

The T in TGROW stands for topic – what your coachee wants to talk about. You would imagine that coachees would arrive at least knowing what they want to talk about, wouldn't you? But sometimes they don't. They book a session because they realise that certain things in their life are not how they want them to be but they haven't a clue why. You've probably had a telephone chat with them before they booked the session, which means they've got the idea that coaching could help, but they've no idea how or what they should talk about. Knowing that you want to feel 'happier', 'more content' or 'challenged' is one thing, but how to achieve those things is not always obvious. Your coachee's need to feel 'happier', 'more content' or 'challenged' during their day-to-day life is likely to be overtaken with more pressing matters like children, partners, parents or work, which means that a coaching session could be her only time to consider these issues in detail.

If your coachees are anything like ours, they won't think very much about their session until they are in the car driving to us or knocking on the door. Work targets, to-do lists and everyday distractions will most likely take up that mental space. On top of that, if she hasn't been coached before and doesn't know what to expect, she might also be feeling a little unprepared.

So if your coachee doesn't know exactly what her topic is, should you have tried to pin her down before you met?

Some coaches we've worked with give their coachees questionnaires to complete, asking questions about their background, life dreams/ambitions, what they feel they are putting up with, and asking them to detail what they think stops them from achieving what they want. For us, though, we believe this is a handicap to being a truly authentic coach. When we train our students, we teach them the power of walking into a coaching session with a brand new coachee, knowing virtually nothing about her. This isn't about being clever or showing off how to 'coach with your eyes shut'; this is about coaching in the moment and being authentic. This is the way we practice and, for us, it is much more helpful to a woman than learning about her life's path, secret ambitions or immediate struggles before we meet her.

We prefer that when a coachee sits down in front of us, we know little about her, except her contact details. When a coachee books an appointment, we will ascertain whether coaching is for her, we will find out what she is hoping to achieve from her session (if she knows) and she will give us just a smattering of information – enough to make an informed choice – to make sure we are the right coach for her and that coaching, as a discipline, is what she requires. We steer clear of too much information at this stage. Why? Well, we might be experienced coaches but we are still human, and it is all too tempting to start wondering what issues she might be facing, the types of questions we might ask or how the session might go.

Imagine this: someone phones to say she is wondering whether to stay living in the city or to move to the seaside. You won't be able to stop yourself thinking about your personal view of the city versus the seaside. The crucial point is that the session is not about you, so the fact that you think having theatres and restaurants close by in the city would be great, or that you'd love to walk by the sea every morning, really isn't helpful to your coachee – in fact, those thoughts may get in the way of you being able to listen to your coachee properly. Or suppose your coachee tells you in advance about a terrible problem she is having at work – might you be tempted to work out a solution (that is *your* solution) for her before the session?

The key to stopping our minds from wandering into that territory is to not know the information before the session. Another issue to consider is that your coachee is probably already overwhelmed with things to do. We believe that filling in forms is likely to aggravate her further. Instead, her coach should be seen as the one person in her life who doesn't demand anything of her. So, avoid becoming another item on her to-do list by not sending her forms to fill in – or risk your coachee deciding she hasn't got time for your form-filling and cancelling her session.

If you are new to coaching, we understand that knowing what your coachee is going to talk about may seem hugely reassuring, but believe us, you are better coming to the session fresh and with no agenda.

Something else you are also better off without is a list of coaching questions by your side for if you get stuck! That is like having *The Highway Code* on the passenger seat while driving at 70 miles per hour on the M25, just in case you need to remember what a sign means … you'll crash – it's as simple as that. We've had students who want a crib sheet of possible coaching questions to hand, particularly if they are coaching over the phone and the coachee can't see it! A list of questions is not just useless, it is absolutely fatal.

Imagine the scene:

COACHEE: I have to decide whether I should sell up and move to a different area. (*Coach thinks 'I'm sure I saw a good question about making decisions somewhere on this page … help where is it?' … Embarrassing silence ensues.*)

COACHEE: Hello?

COACH: Oh sorry, yes I'm here, I was just looking for a good question.

The coachee is left wondering what has happened to her coach and the coach has lost the opportunity to respond to her naturally. Also remember Key Principle 1 – she doesn't want the same questions your other coachees get. She wants a relationship with you based on personal interaction, genuine interest and a coaching session that fits her requirements and circumstances – she won't tolerate anything less.

Student coaches also feel they want to 'prepare'. Here's a tip: there's nothing to prepare! The only preparation you need is this:

- Make sure you won't be disturbed for the duration of the session.

- Clear your mind of your own issues, arguments, mental to-do lists or worries. This is not your time – this is your coachee's time.

- The only materials you need to bring to the session are a pencil and a piece of paper to write down key words or a few notes as you go through the session (read further on for tips on taking notes).

That's it. Your coachees will often ask what preparation they need to do before the session. Again, the answer is very little. The only guidance we give is that they could arrive with an idea of what they want to talk about and what they would like to get from the session, although we'd rather they didn't feed that back to us until the actual appointment. So to summarise: preparation for both coachee and coach is minimal. Remember, coaching is a live process and can only happen during and after the session itself.

Now we can focus on the TGROW model itself.

Topic versus goal

The first major level of understanding with the TGROW model is to recognise the difference between T (topic) and G (goal). You'd think they'd be completely different, wouldn't you? Yet you might be surprised how they can melt seamlessly together at the start of a coaching session without due care and attention.

Keeping these two issues distinct from one another is a major tip for using the TGROW model expertly. These two words set the scene for the rest of your coaching session and without being clear about the difference between them you may well feel in the wilderness, and get lost in there too. By keeping them separate, by retaining their true meaning, you will be building a path directly out of that wilderness for your coachee (and you) to walk on confidently.

The Topic

When we sit with a coachee at their first coaching session, our initial question will be something along the lines of:

▎ **'So, what would you like to talk about today?'**

As a coach, what you are after here is a topic for the session. But ask any woman that question and you are likely to get a barrage of issues: things that have gone wrong, decisions that have implications and people to consider – they will all be thrown at you. In our experience, this opening is perfect for a woman and, typically, she will be expressing Key Principle 4 to the max! She is likely to divulge her frustrations, what gets on her nerves, what she likes, what her hopes are … all in about five minutes flat. Remember, women are masters of communication, so a woman can say a lot in five minutes. That first question means 'I'm going to listen to you' or 'I'm focusing just on you.' It is often a huge relief to know that. Coaching is, of course, more than just offloading or moaning, and this part of the TGROW model will account for just a small percentage of the hour your coachee is with you, but don't underestimate its importance or its ability to set the scene for you.

It is true that some coachees will have thought carefully about which subject to bring to the session and they will give you just one main concern to deal with. For other women, there will be several possible topics and they will all seem to have equal importance. Your job is to help your coachee choose which of those topics to focus on for the session. Generally your session will last an hour; to be productive in that hour, you have to be direct, concise and to the point. That is your job, to keep your coachee focused on the topic and thereby the goal for the session. Choosing the topic, we realise, can be easier said than done. So, here is a great line of questioning which will help you and your coachee immensely:

COACH: So what would you like to talk about today?

COACHEE: Ah, now there's a question. Where to start? Well, my boss has been putting me under enormous pressure of late. To be fair I think she's under a lot of pressure herself, but it means that she's passing more work on to me and she's gone from being approachable to short tempered, so talking to her is difficult. Now that she's in the office less, she's on the road so much more, so I'm left to my own devices to prioritise the work she gives me and I have little direction from her. It seems whichever decision I make it's always the wrong one. I'm tearful too, so when I get home, I take it out on the children, which I hate. They don't understand but they're not sleeping well right now and then I get cross with them. My mother-in-law is great, she's helping a lot, but honestly she makes me feel so bad when I lose my temper with the children. She can be quite judgemental and I know she thinks I should deal with them differently, which makes me even more cross. She didn't have a full-time job to hold down when she was raising her children, the pressure is different now. What else? ... Well, I'm not happy with my weight at the moment, I eat all the wrong things when I'm stressed and I haven't had time to go to the gym, which really annoys me as I normally cope better with stress than this when I'm exercising.

COACH: There's a lot going on right now isn't there?

COACHEE: Yes, I know, this has been building up for over a year now. It's got more and more stressful and now I don't feel I'm doing anything very well. I'm completely overwhelmed and have no idea where to start.

COACH: OK. Well, as you were talking I was just making a bit of a list of what you were telling me. Would it be helpful to read that list back to you, so we can work out the best way to tackle this today?

COACHEE: Sounds like a good idea

COACH: OK, here's what I wrote (showing coachee the list):

- Dealing with stress a little better
- Communicating better with your boss
- Prioritising your workload

- Coping differently with feeling tearful
- Dealing with the children's sleeping pattern
- Finding a different way to react to/interact with your mother-in-law
- You mentioned you'd like to lose weight
- You mentioned your diet and that you know you're eating the wrong things
- You mentioned that exercise usually makes you deal with stress better

COACHEE: Wow, I hadn't realised there was so much.

COACH: If we were to be able to talk about just one of those things in detail today, which one would seem to make sense?

COACHEE: Oh goodness knows, I have no idea. They're all important.

COACH: Well, if we were to imagine that you were to leave here today feeling like a weight had been lifted, if you left with a plan on how to deal with something more effectively, what would make you feel like you'd really made progress?

COACHEE: Do you know, I think if I felt I had more support at home, I actually think I'd cope with the stress at work better. Everything to do with the children is left to me – my partner asks me all the time if it's OK for them to stay up later or what I want them to eat for dinner, which is all very well, but he's not taking responsibility. It's just another thing which comes down to me.

COACH: OK, so out of everything we mentioned above, if you felt like you had more support at home that would be good?

COACHEE: Yes!

So what did you notice about how in this example the coach helped the coachee to choose just one topic?

Well, the first thing the coach did was to ask a question and then just let the coachee talk. She talked and talked, airing everything on her mind.

The coach's second question 'There's a lot going on right now isn't there?' really says 'I'm listening to you.' That one line equals acknowledgement. It tells the coachee that you are taking her seriously. Just knowing that much is often worth its weight in gold. That question was the one that encouraged the coachee to speak more. The coach learnt in the next sentence how long her stress had been going on for and how she is feeling on a deeper level. Does the coach need to know how long her coachee has been under this stress? Not really: it is helpful to understand whether this is a twenty year history or a two month isolated pressure, but don't forget we are not here to diagnose, so how long it has been going on is of minimal importance. Our concern is that, at this moment in time, our coachee is feeling overwhelmed and stressed.

By the coach's third question, she is looking to make sense of all the information that has been given to her so far and, in doing so, her aim is to help the coachee make sense of that information too. Throughout, the coach has been jotting down words to remind her of what the coachee has been saying. She will no doubt have developed her own shorthand to be able to do this discreetly, so it doesn't interrupt the coachee's flow. She will also have practised writing and making eye contact with the coachee at the same time, so the coachee will *not* have been talking to the top of the coach's head! Some of our student coaches find it really helpful to practise this note taking technique while watching the news. The idea is that you watch the news and jot down key words that mean you could tell someone else what happened once the broadcast has finished. This doesn't mean that the coach is secretively making notes about her coachee; it is a way of not forgetting something that may be of importance later in the session.

What you will also notice about the coach's third question is that she asks if it would be helpful to review everything the coachee has mentioned. In this example, the coachee said yes; another coachee may well say no. In this case, our next question would be:

> **'No problem, tell me a bit more about some of the main issues you've already mentioned.'**

What that question would do is get your coachee to open up a bit and give you more information about the main issues (whatever the coachee decides are the most important issues) with a view to you, the coach, being able to help her to funnel down towards concentrating on just one issue for the duration of the session.

Don't forget, every person's mind works differently. Just because you think you know exactly where you would start if you were in her position, that does not mean your coachee should choose the same starting place.

You will see that during the coach's fourth question, she is showing her coachee the piece of paper she has written on – that's really important. Don't forget Key Principle 5 – women tend to experience the world visually first, so seeing her life on paper is likely to help her make sense of where to start. When she sees a set of issues presented in black and white it can highlight where she needs to begin or what might be causing her the most pressure.

By the coach's fifth question, she's asking the coachee to narrow down that list of issues to focus on just one. This is imperative. You cannot coach a coachee on more than one topic at a time. Always ask them which issue seems of most importance and guide them only towards funnelling down – do not guide them towards any particular issue or suggest that if they started in a certain place it would make sense. That would be giving advice which, as you will know by the end of this book, is strictly off limits.

Interestingly, the coachee has no idea how to choose which topic to focus on at this point. She tells the coach they are all important. This is the coach's next question:

> **'Well, if we were to imagine that you were to leave here today feeling like a weight had been lifted, if you left with a plan on how to deal with something more effectively, what would make you feel like you'd really made progress?'**

We love questions like this because they give all the power to the coachee. As coaches, we are not suggesting choosing for them or directing them towards a particular place, but simply directing them towards making a choice of some kind. What came next from the coachee was interesting – an option that had not been mentioned before. Again this is a great example of giving the coachee space to talk. She didn't choose something off the list; she chose something she hadn't at that point mentioned. Her line of thinking was prompted by the coach's fifth question and the thought of leaving the session feeling like a weight had been lifted.

The coach's final question was about checking that she had understood correctly –giving the coachee the opportunity to change her mind and ensure that if our coachee left with a plan to help her feel more supported at home, that would be a good outcome. So now we have our topic: how to feel more supported at home.

So, just to review, here are some guidelines for choosing the topic:

- Ask questions that promote the coachee talking to you and explaining their situation.

- If your coachee doesn't have a specific topic in mind, the above will be of paramount importance. If they already have a topic, ask questions that will give you information about how that topic relates to the rest of their lives.

- Jot down bullet points of the issues your coachee mentions and learn how to do this without looking at your piece of paper.

- With the aid of the funnelling technique, help your coachee to choose just one topic for the session.

The Goal

As we mentioned above, the difference between a topic and a goal should be clear but all too often gets muddled. The topic is what your coachee chooses to talk about, while the goal is where she'd like to end up by the end of the session. This goal may be a small step towards a short, medium or long term life goal which relates to the topic. For instance:

The topic = a desire to live and work in another country

A long term goal = to run your own hotel in Spain

A medium term goal = to move to Spain and get a job managing a hotel for someone else

A short term goal = to take a month off to go to Spain to make contacts in the hotel industry

A goal for your coaching session = to come up with five action points which would help you to start to make your short term goal a reality

This is a manageable goal for the session and your coachee will leave knowing that she has started on the path towards her long term goal. Spending an hour talking around her topic – living and working abroad – would just be a repetition of issues she has already thought about. The focus of a specific, action orientated and forward looking manageable goal for the session means she achieves something tangible and helpful to go away with.

As we've observed, the waters between a topic and a goal can become very easily blurred, especially for new coaches, so we will clarify exactly why and how you can steer your coachee towards a goal for the session. (Please note, we are only steering the coachee towards *a* goal, not any particular goal.)

In short, without a goal, you have nothing to aim for. Without a net on a netball court, how would the players know they'd scored a point? If you get in your car and start driving with no destination in mind, how do you know you've arrived? A coaching session is the same, and this is what stops it ending up just like any other conversation your coachee may have with her friends, her mother, her partner or her siblings. This needs to be different: your coachee is having coaching because she wants to end up somewhere different. The goal for the session is what enables her to do this.

Before we illustrate how to go about helping your coachee define a goal for her session there are two ground rules to be aware of:

1   A goal must be about the coachee herself. A goal is not about getting anyone else around her to react or act differently. You can only coach the woman in front of you and so the goal *must* focus on her.

2   The goal must be measurable. A goal which isn't measurable simply isn't a strong enough goal for a coaching session. There are various ways to measure a goal and we will go into those ways below.

Ground Rule Number 1: Finding an appropriate goal

So, you are back in the room with your coachee. In our previous example, she has decided that her topic for the session is to talk about 'How to feel more supported at home'. Now we need to help her turn that into a measurable goal for the session that focuses on her, and her actions, alone.

Here is a great example of how we'd go about doing that:

COACH (Q1): OK, so we have your topic for today – tell me a bit more about it.

COACHEE: Well, as I was saying, my partner tends to leave all of the responsibility of everything at home to me and I feel I'm lacking any support. It wasn't so bad before my job got busier or before my daughter's sleep pattern went astray. I just know I'm starting to resent the fact that he still puts all the pressure and responsibility of finding the answers onto me. I'm completely unsupported.

COACH (Q2): You've mentioned feeling unsupported several times. Can you tell me what you mean by that exactly?

COACHEE: I mean that he doesn't support me in making the actual decisions. He just goes along with whatever I decide.

COACH (Q3): So he supports you after the decision has been made but the decision is made on your own without support or input from him?

COACHEE: Oh yes, he supports me once I've made a decision – he does back me up, especially if I say no to something my daughter wants – but I need more back-up to actually make the decisions!

COACH (Q4): OK, so if your topic today is about how to feel more supported at home and we could break that down into a goal for today's session, what would that goal be?

COACHEE: Err ... well, I guess it would be to find a way to make him more aware of how unsupported I really feel during the decision making process. If he behaved differently during that part, I'd be much happier.

COACH (Q5): If we were to turn that into a goal *for you* today, how would you reframe that?

COACHEE: A goal for me?

COACH (Q6): Yes, today's session is about you and how you can deal with things differently. It's difficult to try to change someone else or their behaviour, so we can only ever coach on how *you* choose to react or change your behaviour/thinking patterns. So if you were to make a goal based on *you* today, how would you phrase that?

COACHEE: Well … I guess it would be 'to plan how I can communicate that I need more support during the decision making process'.

COACH (Q7): OK, so if today we were to come up with a plan that meant you could explain that you need more support during the decision making process, that would be a good and ethical goal?

COACHEE: That would be great! I honestly believe it would make a big difference to us as a couple and me as an individual actually, so yes … that would be perfect.

Let's look at the coach's first response (Q1). She is asking for more information. Her coachee hasn't told her very much about her frustrations with her partner, so it would be difficult to help the coachee turn her topic into a goal without more information. In return, her coachee tells her how she feels unsupported and expands on her situation.

The coach's second response (Q2) picks up that her coachee has used the word 'unsupported' several times and asks her to explain what she means. It sounds like a fairly obvious question on the face of it, but what you *think* your coachee means and what your coachee *actually* means can be two completely different things. In fact, we've had coachees who, through being coached, have realised that their spouses attach entirely different personal meanings to some of the most obvious words. One coachee had a totally different meaning to the word 'provide' than her husband, which had been the root of a long standing argument for as long as she could remember. It was this exact question in her coaching session that led to the two of them being able to move forwards. If a husband and wife team who have been married for many years get confused over the meanings attached to the same word, then you can see how important it is for a coach who has only just met her coachee to check this too. In this scenario, the coach is clearly listening to exactly what her coachee is saying, presuming nothing and taking nothing for granted.

The result of that question is that the coachee is able to distinguish between when her partner gives her support and when he doesn't. In the midst of emotional tension, it is easy to tar everything with the same brush, creating huge sweeping statements such as 'everything is awful' or 'life is so stressful', when, in fact, it may be a small part of 'everything' or 'life' that is actually causing stress, and the rest of it may be OK. At this point, the coachee was able to pinpoint exactly when she needed more support.

The coach's third statement (Q3), clarifies again what she has heard. It is important that both coach and coachee are on the same page at each stage of the session. If the coach gets confused, or doesn't quite understand what her coachee means, it is absolutely fine and very important, in fact, to go back a step and clarify what is being said. The coach could also have said:

▌ **'Sorry I'm not sure I understood that, can you tell me again?'**

or

▌ **'So are you saying …?'**

When you start coaching more, you will understand the value of clarifying things at each stage and you will soon come up with your own way of phrasing your questions. The main point is not to be afraid to ask the question – after all, this is coaching, not telepathy!

By Q4, the coach is taking the coachee back to their topic and asking them how they would reframe that into a goal for the session. This is about keeping your coachee on track. It is very easy for coachees to get sidelined when they are telling you the in's and out's of the story. For the purposes of our example, we are keeping the coachee's answers pretty much to the point, but in a real situation you will find that one story can lead on to another story which can lead onto another issue. Your job is to keep bringing the coachee back to the topic for the session, checking that she is still talking about the topic she feels is important for that session and asking her to frame that topic into a goal for the session.

By Q5, the coach has recognised that, given the opportunity, the coachee would really like to alter the behaviour of her partner, so she flags up to her that it is only *her* reaction to her partner's behaviour that she can control, and so she asks her to reframe her goal into one specifically for her. Remember Ground Rule 1: the goal *must* be about the coachee herself and never about anyone else. We cannot change the behaviour of others, only ourselves.

In Q6, the coach explains exactly what she means. Not everyone you coach will be familiar with what a goal is supposed to look like or how to frame a goal, so part of your job is to coax the coachee in the direction of making a good quality goal. Remember, it is the quality of the goal we are looking at here, not which goal. We are not pushing, leading or promoting any one particular goal, simply that it must be aligned to the coachee and no one else.

By Q7, the coach has checked her coachee is happy and content with her chosen goal. It has been reframed in a way that is pertinent to the coachee, which means that with her permission, the coach can move on to measuring the goal.

Ground Rule Number 2: Measure your coachee's goal

A goal can be measured in several different ways. The most popular among our students and with our coachees is the 1–10 score. You ask your coachee to measure where they currently feel they are in terms of their chosen goal and where they would like to be by the end of the session. If you use this method, your conversation would run along these lines:

COACH: If you were to choose a number between 1 and 10 on how near you feel to having a plan to explain to your partner that you want support during the decision making process, with 1 being having no plan at all and 10 knowing exactly what you want to say, where would you say you are?

COACHEE: About a 4.

COACH: OK, so that's less than halfway. If we were to raise that figure up a little by the end of this session would that feel good?

COACHEE: Absolutely.

COACH: What number would be a good number to raise it to?

COACHEE: If we got to a 7, I think I'd feel prepared enough to know how to deal with this and ultimately I'd cope with the stress at work better I think.

It is important when using this measurement that you don't presume your coachee needs to, or wants to, reach the golden 10 in forty minutes flat. That might be how long you have left in your coaching session with them that day, so to move from a 4 to a 10 is a pretty big ask. Coachees often feel that a slight upwards movement is all they need to make themselves feel more in control, or less stressed, with a situation. Also, a coachee often needs to reflect on what happened during the session afterwards. Our coachees often say they need to go away and practise something we've talked about before they can say they've truly reached a 10.

Do make sure that you and your coachee are measuring the same thing; that is, where they are *in relation to the specific goal they have set for that session*. If the 1–10 measurement feels awkward, find another measure. There are many other imaginative measuring scales to use and they will be based on the information the coachees give you. For instance, for a coachee who has spoken about the enormity of her issue feeling as though she is trying to climb a mountain, you might feel comfortable using a measuring scale of how far up that mountain she thinks she currently is and where she'd like to be by the end of the session. With a coachee who equates their topic or issue with needing to get further up the ladder, you might ask how many rungs their ladder has and how far up the ladder they are already. Another creative measure we've seen used by a student, David Edwards, was how fog-bound a coachee felt. This individual had mentioned feeling 'in a fog' and so David asked how fog-bound she felt; that is, what they could see. By the end of the session, David asked again how fog-bound they were and the coachee reported being able to see clearly as the sun was out!

Another of our students, James Carter, started to use a great question when his coachees measured where they were on a scale of 1–10. If his coachee gave him a particularly low score, such as a 1 or 2, he'd ask, 'So what stops that figure being a minus?'. We've seen his coachees' moods shift instantly from being quite low about their situation to starting to understand why it is as high as a 1 or a 2 – it is a perspective that can work very effectively.

Remember: our minds are hugely creative and most women are particularly visual (Key Principle 5), so they are able to come up with images that are unique to them. Use those images and work with them for their own personal measuring tool.

The idea is that your coachee leaves the session seeing some progress: you are measuring so the coachee can see that she has moved forward, so the measuring is for her benefit. It would not be ethically sound for you to constantly measure what a great coach you were in terms of how far your coachees move forwards! This is not about you, it is about your coachee and their personal advancement. We all like to see how far we've moved forwards, don't we? Have you ever used a pedometer for instance? When they first became popular, everyone seemed to have one and was counting the steps they had taken each day. What about when people set the mileage gauge before they leave for a long journey so they can chart how many miles they've driven? We all like to see movement and this is the coaching way, so even if your coachee moves just one point up the scale, knowing that they have advanced gives them a lift and the confidence to know that change is possible.

Another way to use the 1–10 scale is to use it throughout the TGROW model. If your coachee starts at a 6 for instance, one of your first questions could be, 'What would you need to do to reach a 7?' Then a little way into the coaching session, you'd recap what you had both discussed your coachee would need to do and then say, 'OK, so imagine if you'd done that and you were at a strong 7 now – how would you go up to an 8?' It is a steady way of moving your coachee up through the scale in stages.

This is the magic of setting a goal for the session. If both you and your coachee know exactly what she wants to get out of your time together, you will concentrate and stay focused. If your coachee starts to get sidetracked, you will have a very clear objective to bring her back to. Our students sometimes wonder if they are allowed to interrupt a coachee. Interrupting is to be used carefully: if you interject all the time you wouldn't be listening or giving your coachee room to think or speak. However, an interruption to bring your coachee back to the goal or the topic for the session – to interrupt with respect in order to clarify what they mean – is sometimes necessary. Because your coachee has specified where she wants to get to before she leaves, it is fine to butt in if she starts to talk about something else. What we ask is that you use this with care and attention.

Here's what we mean:

> **'Can I just check how talking about your mother's best friend will help you to get to your goal for today?'**

or

> ■ **'Could I just bring you back to the goal for today's session.'**

or even

> ■ **'We have around 20 minutes of the session left, would it be OK to summarise where we are now?'**

All of these questions are appropriate 'interrupting' questions that will break a coachee's stream and give the coach an opportunity to check they are making progress in a way that will benefit the coachee's end goal.

Remember, if there is a clear goal, then all your coachee's energy will be directed towards it. By the end of the session, the stress she was feeling about her situation will be lessened because, instead of just moaning about it, she will actually be doing something to change it.

Seeing that she is doing something which is directed towards the change she wants will help her feel stronger, resulting in more confidence and a higher self value. We see it every single day; you will too if you are already coaching. By becoming proactive in their own goals and working towards them steadily, your coachees will be more in control of their own lives.

Another important element to helping your coachee choose an appropriate goal is to listen to the language they use to describe that goal. This is really important. Think about New Year and how frequently New Year resolutions get broken before the end of January. Many resolutions don't last because they are framed in negative language using sentences that start: 'I'll lose ...' or 'I'll give up ... 'or 'I'll try to ...'

Hardly very inspiring. It is simply not convincing if your coachee says:

> ■ **'I'll try not to check my e-mails so much.'**

Would you believe her? No, neither would we! However, if your coachee's goal was to:

> **'Come up with a schedule that involves reading my e-mails twice a day'**

we would be much more convinced she means business, and she is more likely to come up with a plan and work with it. What's the difference? Well, in the first example our coachee is telling us what she is 'not' going to do. This automatically puts her unconscious mind in a state of 'lacking' something. It is not positive, plus the word 'try' indicates some reluctance to stick to it or believe that she could actually train herself to look at her e-mails less. The word 'try' is a classic giveaway. On the other hand, our second example has a strategy to it: she has ascertained that her e-mails are an issue and she knows she has to look at them twice a day, so she plans to put a structure in place that enables her to do that effectively. Now that's a goal.

But the language of goals doesn't stop there. Putting a goal into the future doesn't help either. For instance:

> **'I'll give up biscuits tomorrow'**

gives that same feeling of 'I'm going to miss out on something.' It is framed negatively for one, but it is also set in the future. We all know that tomorrow never comes and by telling ourselves that we have 'one more day' is simply playing mind games that we will never win. So, what would be a sturdier, more positive goal?

> **'I enjoy eating healthy food every day.'**

This does it for us. It is motivating, it starts now and it doesn't imply a 'lack' of anything – your coachees are much more likely to enjoy working with this goal.

There are a few ways to remind you how to help your coachees structure their goals in the right way (you will find templates for these on the accompanying CD). During your training, we advise that you visit these acronyms and find one that means something to you; but remember what we said above about writing things down during a session and walking into your coaching room with an armful of notes. You are not going to be an effective coach if you are referring to anything on paper. What you need is an effective way to remember when you are 'in the moment' with your coachee for when the G part of the TGROW model comes into play, so commit these to memory.

SMART and FEMALE

We use two acronyms. The first one is an old favourite – SMART. You will no doubt have heard of this before as it is extremely effective and makes sure that your coachee's goal is a strong one. The other one we've formed through our research on how a woman thinks – FEMALE.

First of all, we will talk you through SMART:

S stands for **S**pecific (because narrowing focus increases effectiveness)

M stands for **M**easurable (a reminder to measure the goal so you know when you've reached it)

A stands for **A**ction orientated (What actions will your coachee take?)

A stands for **A**ttractive (Is the end result really attractive to your coachee?)

A stands for **A**chievable (Is the goal achievable to reach an outcome during the session?)

R stands for **R**ealistic (Does your coachee believe this goal is achievable for them outside of the session?)

T stands for **T**ime phased (What will your coachee do and when?)

Taking the goal in our initial example,

> **'How I can communicate that I need more support during the decision making process?'**

Let's check it against SMART:

Is it Specific?
Yes, the coachee knows she wants a plan and has been specific in where she needs the support.

Is it Measurable?

Yes, we've already started to measure the goal in our example using the 1–10 scale. We will be able to chart her progress throughout the session using that scale by checking what figure she feels she is on from time to time.

Is it Action orientated?

Yes, the coachee is willing to come up with actions to carry out her goal.

Is it Achievable?

Yes, there is no reason why she shouldn't be able to plan this during her session, especially with a coach who keeps her on track and focused throughout.

Is it Attractive?

Yes, she has said that achieving this goal will improve her life at home and her relationship with her husband.

Is it Realistic?

Yes, our coachee believes this will be realistic for her to achieve when she gets back home.

Is it Time phased?

Yes, as her coach, you will summarise at the end of the session and ask her *when* she will be able to take action on her plan. The plan will have a time frame written into it.

So, now onto our acronym FEMALE:

F   stands for **F**ocused (she is focused on being able to take positive steps towards that one goal alone)

E   stands for **E**mpowered (she is taking ownership of the goal, which is to do with her and no one else)

M   stands for **M**easured (she is able to find a scale of measurement that fits her style in order to understand how close she is to attaining her goal)

A   stands for **A**ligned to her ethics and beliefs (she is able to articulate how the goal runs alongside those ethics and beliefs that she holds dear)

L/E   stands for **L**inked to her **E**motionally (that she has bought into her goal emotionally and has made a link between the practical solution oriented steps and the reasons *why* she would take those steps)

Now let's test our coachee's goal against the acronym:

Is it Focused?

Yes, our coachee is sure that this is an appropriate goal to run with for the session and she is focused on getting a solution.

Is it Empowered?

Yes, the coach has made sure that our coachee has a goal which is particular to her, that affects her behaviour and consequently will empower her to take action.

Is it Measured?

Yes, as we saw before, the coach has already started to measure the goal.

Is it Aligned?

Yes, through the checking process in Q7 the coach has ascertained that this goal hasn't gone against her ethics or beliefs. If a coachee has been led in any way towards a particular goal there is likely to be incongruence between the goal and her ethics or beliefs. A woman's beliefs (although she is unlikely to shout about them all the time) will be very deeply ingrained and so a goal has to feel comfortable and be in line with those principles for her to make positive steps towards it.

Is it Linked to her Emotionally?

For any woman to 'buy into' her own goal, she needs to know there is an emotional link to that goal. This isn't to say that a woman and her goals won't be strategic, businesslike or professional, it is simply that without an emotional pay-off of some description, without a definite link between the goal and how she feels about it, her goal may fail. In the case of our coachee, she has made a link between the goal itself (i.e. How I can communicate that I need more support during the decision making process?) and the emotion behind it (i.e. I honestly believe it would make a big difference to us as a couple and me as an individual).

Becoming familiar with this mnemonic will mean that you automatically do a quick mental check on your coachee's goal to see if it is SMART and/or FEMALE. Usually if your coachee's goal isn't SMART or FEMALE, it is because it isn't specific enough.

So, just to review, here are some guidelines for formulating the goal:

- Make sure that the goal is in the present tense.

- Ensure that the goal is concerned with the coachee herself and no one else.

- Review the language the goal has been framed in – it must be positive and in the present tense.

- Use a tool to measure how your coachee feels in relation to the goal. Measure at the beginning, midway through (at least once) and again at the end to see visible growth and movement.

So, T and G are the first stepping stones on your pathway to a successful outcome in a coaching session. So now you understand what they are and how to use them, you are ready to move along TGROW to R – the reality.

Reality

We often refer to reality as the 'comfort zone' of the student coach. This part of the TGROW model is all about finding out what is happening for the coachee right now – the reality of the situation they find themselves in. This is a prime time for the coach to start understanding on a deeper level how the topic affects the coachee on a day-to-day basis. It is in this section that the coachee will be able to explain the complexities as she sees them. Your aim as a coach is to get your coachee talking. Often when we explain what happens in our lives to a complete stranger, or someone just on the periphery of our lives, we see for ourselves the patterns and the repetitions we display unconsciously.

Have you ever heard the saying, 'If you always do what you've always done, you'll always get what you've always got'? Well, we all know it is true and we all know that the only way to change is to change our own behaviour. How do we do that though? This is where asking your coachee to explain the reality of their situation can help. We first have to identify what we do in a particular situation. Most of us develop patterns of behaviour over the years, usually based on our previous experiences, personality, strengths and weaknesses. What your coachees might well find is that they repeat the same behaviours each time a similar situation occurs. We are often very reactionary and completely unaware that we do this. Once we recognise those patterns, however, we can then choose which ones to change (if they are no longer serving us well) and which ones to keep.

Here's what we mean:

COACH: OK, so we've established our goal for the session. Tell me a bit more about the situation?

COACHEE: Right, well, I suppose he's never really made many decisions in our relationship, they're always down to me. It's not that he shirks responsibility or anything but he has a stressful job – he tends to get quite stressed actually. I suppose I've taken on the role of making decisions at home so that he doesn't have to. It's been my way of supporting him really. I mean, if he's had a really stressful day, he'll come home and either be quite quiet and just sit in front of the telly or he'll go on and on about the situation at work and what happened, what he's worried about and so on – the last thing he needs is extra responsibility at home, so I guess, really, I've made the decisions. I've tried to make life outside of work as easy as possible for him. I've never actually asked him to make any decisions ... *(pause)* In fact, half the time he doesn't even know about the decisions I make! *(laughs)* If only he knew what goes on behind the scenes to make everything slot into place and appear perfectly normal! He doesn't really have any idea of what I do to smooth the path. If I make a decision about anything to do with our social life or where the children are going, there's no real point in telling him half the time ... until the actual day, that is; he won't remember and it's just not on his radar. It's usually the day of the event that I'll tell him what's happening. *(laughs again)* I'll tell him that we're going out somewhere or having someone over, or that the kids have got a play date – he won't mind whether they have a play date or not but he wouldn't think to arrange it or anything. I'll do that with the other mums and then just tell him where to drop them off when the day comes.

COACH: You seem to have made a conscious decision yourself to make the household decisions as your way of supporting your husband in what can be quite a stressful job, is that right?

COACHEE: Yes, I have ... I hadn't really realised I'd done that actually. I did make that decision some time ago, and I stand by it too. I do like being able to support him and think it's right that he doesn't have the worry about what the kids are doing, where we're going and so on. He's very easy going when he's relaxed and happy and I'd rather do what I can to support him.

So what did you learn?

With just one question and one clarifying statement look how much information the coach has got from her coachee. Not only has she established more about how their relationship works, she has also established that it was the coachee herself who engineered the way their relationships works and took on the role of making decisions – for the express purpose of helping to keep her husband's stress levels down. We've established that she prefers to work in this way and that it seems to work for the household. What the rest of the session will need to focus on is her goal, which may include what aspects of that previous decision are no longer working for her and how the coachee thinks she will be able to manoeuvre her original decision to fit with the person she is now and the work commitments she has now.

Coaches and student coaches beware: don't allow yourself or your coachee to become too comfortable in the R part of this model. We don't call it the comfort zone for nothing. Sitting and listening to a coachee's reality is interesting, but it doesn't stretch the coach and it doesn't stretch the coachee. Given half a chance the coachee probably would stay in the R of the model for some time – it is where she knows, it is the part of the model that her friends and family use with her, it is her letting off steam mode, it is her release and, trust us, she can feel *tons* better for just having sat in the R part of the model for the whole hour. But that is not your job as a coach – if you let your coachee stay in R you are effectively a very expensive friend! The fact that you are a coach means that the conversation moves beyond the organised moan, beyond the reality and up into O, the options, which is where we will go now.

Options

In our experience, the options area often gets ignored by student coaches and it is also all too easy to ignore the O as an experienced coach. An exceptional coach, however, will plug the O and keep on plugging the O – pushing their coachee for more and more ideas. Ask anybody what they can do about a situation and they will reel off a list of things they've tried, things their family or friends have suggested, things that didn't work, things they were going to do but for some reason didn't. But that is not what you as a professional and exceptional coach are after. What you want are the options that your coachee *hasn't* thought of before, the options they previously threw out as unrealistic or ridiculous. You want to expand your coachee's notion of what is and isn't possible. Here's what we mean:

COACH (Q1): So, we seem to have a situation where you made a decision to take on all the family decision making, so your husband had less day-to-day stress?

COACHEE: Yes.

COACH (Q2): But I'm also hearing that the reason we're here today is because your stress at work has increased, and now the stress of making family decisions on your own and without any input from your husband is overwhelming and makes you feel unsupported, is that right?

COACHEE: Totally.

COACH (Q3): OK, so, let's say you could stand by your original decision yet at the same time communicate to your husband that you now feel unsupported – what would you do?

COACHEE: No idea!

COACH (Q4): If you did one thing this evening differently that would make a difference, what would it be?

COACHEE: Well, when the kids ask something, I could say 'Ask your dad!' After all he says 'Ask your mum!' That could work.

COACH (Q5): What else could work?

COACHEE: *(silence)* I'm out of ideas … *(pause)* I think I make decisions without realising sometimes. And then I get cross when I realise my husband has had no input and I've taken care of everything on my own again.

COACH (Q6): How do you know you're making decisions?

COACHEE:	Because my shoulders immediately tense up and I feel cross. It's because I don't feel supported ... yet, of course, I carry on making decisions and not saying anything.
COACH (Q7):	If you were to do something completely different what would you do?
COACHEE:	I'd give my husband an in-tray.
COACH (Q8):	An in-tray?
COACHEE:	Yep! Mostly there's a piece of paperwork for most of the decisions I make around the house and with the children – there's permission slips, party invites, bills to pay, forms to fill in, etc. If he had an in-tray I could put some of them in there and let him deal with them.
COACH (Q9):	How would that affect your goal for today?
COACHEE:	Well, I'd be communicating to my husband that I'd like his input more. I could talk to him about it and tell him where his in-tray was and ask him to deal with some of the household stuff and decisions instead of me.
COACH (Q10):	What else could you do?
COACHEE:	Pass ... *(pause)* I could use the pinboard in the kitchen differently. If I wrote on there the decisions we needed to still make, then he'd see them too. I wouldn't be walking around keeping them to myself – they wouldn't be clogging up my brain along with everything else – that'd be really helpful.

Let's just take a look at the way the coach used O here:

- Q1 – the coach is clarifying the first half of the coachee's scenario here to check they are on the same page.

- Q2 – the coach continues to clarify the next half of the scenario to make sure they understand each other.

- Q3 – with this question the coach is pushing for options from the coachee. See how the phrasing is positive, with the expectation that the coachee's outcome is entirely workable and realistic.

- Q4 – the coach rephrases an options question, pushing for other alternatives.

- Q5 – this is another question that is promoting thinking outside the box, asking the coachee to dig around for further options.

- Q6 – picking up on the coachee's previous comment about how she often makes decisions without realising it, this question asks her to pinpoint *how* she might know when she is making a decision. Her answer is important because it continues to give the coach more information and also gives the coachee an opportunity to put into words her unconscious behaviour, thereby bringing it to her attention so she can choose to alter it if she thinks it would be suitable.

- Q7 – this is the coach's fourth question that prods the coachee to search for more workable options. By now, this is far beyond what any friend, colleague or associate would push for, but interestingly the coachee's response is completely different to the previous suggestions.

- Q8 – this question clarifies and makes sure that the coach is up to speed with what the coachee means.

- Q9 – this question goes back to the goal and keeps the coachee on track.

- Q10 – finally the coach asks again what else the coachee could do.

In this short scenario, the coach has asked five questions that promote options and clarified the situation three times. One question asks the coachee to pinpoint certain actions in what is usually unconscious behaviour, and the coached flipped back to the goal once to check she is still on track. The pushing for other answers, possibilities and solutions brought up much more information.

The wrong way to do this would have been to stop after the first option question was answered, as in the example below:

COACH (Q1): So, we seem to have a situation where you made a decision to take on all the family decision making, so your husband had less day-to-day stress.

COACHEE: Yes.

COACH (Q2): But I'm also hearing that the reason we're here today is because your stress at work has increased, and now the stress of making family decisions on your own and without any input from your husband is overwhelming and makes you feel unsupported, is that right?

COACHEE: Totally.

COACH (Q3): OK, so let's say you could seamlessly blend and stand by your original decision yet at the same time communicate to your husband that you now feel unsupported – what would you do?

COACHEE: No idea.

COACH (Q4): If you did one thing this evening differently that would make a difference, what would it be?

COACHEE: Well, when the kids ask something, I could say 'Ask your dad!' After all he says 'Ask your mum!' That could work.

COACH (Q5): Great, that sounds like a plan, well done.

The chances are this particular answer from the coachee is slightly flippant! By accepting that first answer the coach is missing out on vast amounts of information about the coachee and her situation, and it gives absolutely no opportunity for the coachee to move forwards in a different direction. By persistently pushing, digging and probing for further ideas, the coachee is much more likely to think of a solution that would work long term instead of a reactionary short term fix.

We spoke to Marie Chambers about her experience of coaching. Marie is now Managing Director of a successful PR company, but things were quite different when she first visited a coach. She says that the coaching sessions gave her an opportunity to reinvent herself completely and it was all down to coaching's ability to expand her options that brought her true potential to light.

Following a difficult time at work and then a very sudden family death, on her return to work Marie was faced with redundancy. Feeling completely lost, very resentful and utterly unprepared for both her personal and professional situation, she recognised she needed help from someone and took her company's offer of coaching.

Marie explained that at this point she couldn't see a way forward to put any positive shape back into her life. When she started talking to her coach about the options available to her in her professional life, she realised that there were issues in several areas of her life that needed addressing. Her coach dug around and asked her about her personal commitments, life situation, her aspirations, how she saw herself and how she'd like to see herself. He asked her about her strengths, her weaknesses and what changes she needed to make.

She confided in her coach that she'd always had a burning desire to work for herself. Marie realised she had been putting off that big decision and finally decided not only to set up her own business, but to change every area of her life that was no longer working for her. Through her coach's patience, tenacity and skill to draw out more options from her, she changed everything about her situation. Marie says: 'I had to look at every aspect of my life and got rid of the clutter that was holding me back. Coaching helped me to regain my confidence, and see positively how I could improve my career prospects. Coaching wasn't someone telling me what to do but a way for me to identify the key qualities and strengths I had within me to get my life back on track.'

Another common coaching scenario is to find yourself with a woman sitting in front of you (or on the other end of your telephone) with too much choice and too many options. Student coaches can feel overwhelmed by the amount their coachees bring to the session, but with quality training and practice the skills you need to help your coachee focus her options into workable, practical solutions will come.

Sydney Tyler Thomas (www.sydneytylerthomas.com) is one businesswoman who illustrates this perfectly. She is an excellent example of a coachee whose choices and challenges were blocking her ability to move forward. This is Sydney's story of how working over the telephone from the US with her coach Gwen Channer (www.gwenchanner.com) in Australia, for just 30 minutes, moved her from a woman feeling overwhelmed almost to the point of paralysis, to thriving on creativity once more:

> I have a background in small business development consulting and market research. I worked in the corporate sector for many years until I realised that everything about it was killing me! I made the major decision to leave for a simpler, more peaceful life. What I hadn't accounted for, though, was how difficult it would be to find a satisfying job. I began to lose the confidence, creativity and fire that

had always defined me. Eventually I came up with an idea for a new business based on my years of experience reviewing, proofreading and editing documents. I'd been a successful entrepreneur in the past, so I was quite surprised when I seemed to run into a wall getting my new business venture started.

When I saw an offer for a free 30-minute coaching session being offered by a fellow group member on LinkedIn, I took it. To be perfectly honest, I wasn't expecting much, particularly from a 30-minute telephone coaching session, but I decided that I didn't have anything to lose. Gwen Channer was my coach and from the moment the session started, she exuded an air of confidence in herself, and in me, to identify the source of my issue and find workable solutions to address it. It didn't take long to recognise that I was feeling overwhelmed by the enormity of the possibilities before me. I'm a very creative, energetic, entrepreneurial spirit and because I'm woefully underemployed at present, I've had lots of time over the past few months to think about this business and how wonderful it will be to be self-employed again. The problem was that after thinking of business ideas for several hours each day when I couldn't implement them, by the time I got home in the evening and was ready to work on my business, I felt so overwhelmed by the weight of all my ideas that I couldn't figure out where to start.

I told my coach that if I had to illustrate the way I was feeling in a cartoon, it would be an image of an utterly exhausted woman sitting at a desk with a balloon above her head. Inside that balloon there are 10,000 little yellow Post-it notes swirling around, each with a different marketing/business development idea written on it.

One of the things I remember thinking about Gwen at the time was that she had an uncanny ability to help me answer my own questions by gently asking me questions in return. The pivotal point in our session came when I mentioned that I had a small jar that I use to keep track of my various housekeeping projects that I want or need to work on. I write down the project on a slip of paper, put it in the jar, and pull one out when I have some time to focus on one of them.

As we explored a way of harnessing my creativity, that small jar comment morphed into the idea of having five boxes for me to place slips of paper into to help me manage the business ideas that had been swirling around in my head, making me feel overwhelmed, unfocused and unproductive.

After considering several options for distinguishing between the boxes, I decided that I'd have five boxes, one for each of the following: (1) things I can do in 30 minutes or less; (2) things I can do in 60 minutes or less; (3) things I can do in four hours or less (anything that takes longer than four hours probably needs to be broken up into smaller tasks); (4) topics I want to blog or otherwise write about; and (5) ideas for marketing the books that I'm in various stages of self-publishing.

It's encouraging to realise that what I think is an elegantly simple, yet highly effective, tool for me, came from a seed buried somewhere deep inside me, and that Gwen watered that seed and helped it to blossom into something so helpful and positive.

The solution is brilliant and is working beautifully. I'm finding that the benefits go well beyond the obvious. In addition to having all of my ideas written down in a place where I can retrieve them, I'm able to get them out of my head so I don't feel as exhausted or overwhelmed. When I'm ready to work, it's much easier for me to figure out what to do because my options are right there, depending on how much time I want to spend. Perhaps the nicest part of all is the sense of magic, mystery and synchronicity that comes from picking an idea from the box, not knowing which one it will be, but believing that the one I choose will be exactly the one that I'm meant to work on at that particular time – it takes the pressure off of prioritising which idea to work on next.

I'm looking forward to working with Gwen again moving forward. I know that having a coach to help me grow my business is one of the smartest business investments I can make.

Here is another perspective on helping coachees who feel stuck to find further options. When we use this next exercise we are tapping into Key Principle 3 (women have the ability to fix several problems at the same time) and Key Principle 5 (women are able to use visualisation very effectively).

The exercise focuses your coachee on the best outcome they could possibly hope for. This is where imagination, visualisation and placing distance between the here and now and the future means that your coachee's most heartfelt wish list gets aired. We ask:

> **'If you could have your very best outcome, if this situation turned itself around to prove to be the best decision you ever made, what would you be doing?'**

For some, this exercise is known as 'la-la land' – not a very technical term, we'll grant you that, but it is about taking your coachee away from reality for a short time, about getting to the bottom of what they'd really love to see happen with their lives and about projecting their dreams into the future to describe to you what they see, hear, feel and notice. In a corporate situation, the term 'la-la land' won't be appropriate, so you might say:

> **'In an environment with no rules, restrictions and limitations, what would you see evolving?'**

or

> **'If there were no ramifications and you could choose to make any decisions and have any outcome, what would you want?'**

What this does is to move the coachee from the impossible to the possible – it creates possibility where none was thought to exist. This type of forward thinking has worked time and time again for our coachees, enabling them to delve deep into their solution making processes and find out what they'd most like to happen. What you will also notice about this exercise, when you use it in practice, is that your coachee's vision of the future won't only encompass the topics you are talking about – it will shift her thinking sideways and backwards and she will fix other issues right in front of your eyes. You might also notice a coachee's change of stage – they smile, the shoulders relax, they take a deep breath and feel instantly calmer. When someone shifts their state of mind, they can't help but feel differently and it is easier to make good decisions when you are relaxed and calm.

The second part to this exercise is where 'la-la land' meets reality. If you've got a clear picture (your female coachee is likely to have a strong ability to visualise – Key Principle 5) as to what your coachee would most like to see happen, your next line of questioning takes that further:

> **'So what elements of that vision can you bring into the here and now?'**
>
> **'What would that imaginary outcome give you and how can you recreate that feeling today?'**
>
> **'Now we've established what you'd most love to see happening, how do you blend that with reality?'**

These questions all assume that some part of what your coachee most desires can be manifested in the here and now; it is just about unlocking those parts and working out how to put it into practice.

Another exercise perfectly aligned to the female mindset is the film clip exercise. This uses every ounce of your coachee's clever and natural visualisation skills. Just as with any coaching exercise, always ask your coachee's permission, never dictate. The film clip exercise involves the coachee placing her feet firmly on the ground, closing her eyes and visualising the results she most desires. We suggest that when the coach explains how this works, they make the coachee aware that they will keep their eye on the clock and won't leave them there indefinitely with their eyes closed!

Explain that you will give them say 60 seconds to create a short film clip in their mind of exactly how they'd like their situation to pan out. After the 60 seconds, gently tell them that they can open their eyes when they are ready to do so and describe what they visualised. The way to use this exercise to its capacity is for your coachee to bring their images to life – ask them to imagine colour, movement, people talking, places, to notice what is going on around them. This exercise does something very important. It gives the unconscious mind a clear direction. You will learn a little more about the unconscious in this book, but for now, just know that the unconscious is a powerful tool in helping to manifest your desired outcomes. You just have to give it a clear destination, a steady picture of what you want and then it will flag to your conscious mind ideas and events in everyday life to help you get there. You may have heard this technique described as 'cosmic ordering' – the philosophy being that if you quieten and steady your mind, then focus in elaborate detail on the event you want to come to pass, it can come to life. You can effectively order it – cosmically!

The film clip introduces your end destination as reality in your mind long before it becomes actual reality. In her book, *Life is a Gift*, Gill Edwards explains:

> Visualisation is a powerful tool for reality creation. The cosmos will send you whatever matches your vibrations – so if you spend time each day happily daydreaming about your future, you magnetise it towards you. You might imagine a successful job interview, or walking hand in hand with your loved one, or running a marathon, or moving into your new home. The more real it feels, the more strongly you are attracting it. The Universe does not distinguish between a real and imagined experience; it simply responds to your vibrations. If you consistently hold the energy of a future self, then sooner or later, reality *has* to snap into place to match it. (Edwards, 2007: 104)

You are tapping into a technique thousands of years old which has been used by businessmen and women and sports professionals alike; you and your coachees can use it too.

The film clip exercise does something else that seems to work very well for the unconscious – it encourages us to think backwards. In our experience, envisaging a point in time in the future where everything has worked out perfectly and then asking the coachee to work backwards and describe each action it took for them to achieve their goal, seems to be less intimidating than asking them to take a step forwards from today into the future. Try it yourself: create a film clip that is detailed, colourful and specific. Repeat it in your mind when you are still and there are no distractions around you. Afterwards, let your thoughts come back to the here and now and trust that your unconscious will do the rest – it usually does!

So there you have several ways of introducing your coachees to an infinite number of options. Play and creativity come into their own, giving the coachee the opportunity to find answers stored deep in her psyche; they are there, trust us on that one. While we are on the subject of play and creativity, don't pin your coachee down to having to carry out each of her options exactly as she describes them. While there is no pressure to take any of them further, your coachee can take the liberty of going to extremes and proposing things she would never actually do – this in itself stretches her mind and means that more options are expressed. Put undue pressure on her at this stage to take each one seriously and she may censor what she tells you.

The options part of TGROW is about play – stretching her mind, bringing up sensible options and serious realistic contenders alongside outlandish and out of character options. Sometimes it is those options that, when talked about and considered seriously, can be broken down into possibilities that would work in the real world.

Will, When and Why

Finally we have W, which stands for Will, When and Why. The W marks the final part of the TGROW model where you are going to ask for a commitment from your coachee. After everything you've spoken about during their session, after all their ideas have come out (as a result of your probing questions), after your coachee has uncovered a deeper level of understanding of her behaviour and her situation, and after your expectation of positive change, your W is the *Will*.

'So ...' we ask, 'what will you do now?' – it is one of the simplest yet most effective questions to wrap up your coaching session. Unlike a coffee with a friend or a chat with a colleague or indeed a moan with a family member, what you are asking for is some commitment to the possible solutions which have been raised during the session. Said with conviction and expectation, your coachee will take something from the session and agree to put it into action to promote change.

Here are some great questions we would ask during the W of the TGROW model:

> **'To what extent does this course of action meet your objectives?'**
>
> **'On a scale of 1–10 how committed are you to this plan?'**
>
> **'What support do you need?'**
>
> **'Who else will be involved?'**
>
> **'What will you do right now as a first step?'**
>
> **'Where will you be when you do this?'**
>
> **'How will this make you feel different?'**
>
> **'What impact will doing this have on you personally?'**
>
> **'What impact will this have on those around you?'**

Notice they are all information accessing questions – they all wrap up the session and ask for commitment to movement forwards. You could tap into the visual part of the coachee's brain by asking questions that promote her visualising herself making these changes. These steps will cement the impact of the session with your coachee.

When is the next W – when is your coachee going to do what she says? Far from being dictatorial, by asking her to commit to a point in time when she will put her thoughts and ideas into practice, you are giving her the opportunity to make space in what will probably be a very busy schedule. In the quiet and calm of a coaching session, where it genuinely feels as though the world outside has stopped for a while, she can come to a resolution. Once your coachee steps back into her car and drives off, her mobile will be ringing, she will have e-mails to answer, a meeting to attend or children to pick up from school. Without the when, even the best coaching session in the world could mean that the coachee gets too consumed by day-to-day activities to put her well meaning action plan into place. It is your job to help her create the time and space to do that. Most of our coachees will get their diaries out there and then, scheduling phone calls or planning time without the children at home. If plans are diarised, it is commitment and planned action that will change things. Often, previous irritations don't seem to bother our coachees as much once a decision to change has been made and an implementation date has been put in her diary. Psychologically it is progress forward; physically it is movement forward.

The final W stands for *Why*. This is a very important final part of the TGROW model and will help your coachee stick to her plans – remember FEMALE? This is her emotional buy-in. The coaching session is a protected point in time where floating options, solutions and possibilities are safe. What happens though if your coachee has committed to walking three miles every Monday and Thursday after work and the next Thursday it is pouring with rain, she gets stuck in traffic or has a terrible day at work and would rather take a hot bath and eat chocolate in front of the TV? What is actually going to get her to keep to her beautiful plan of walking three miles twice a week? What you are finding out here is what it will take for her to carry out those plans if everything on the day itself seems to be conspiring against her. The why gives validation to the plan. Here is what we would ask:

> **'OK, imagine, you've had the worst day ever, you're tired, hungry and still have the kids to put to bed – what will make you stick to your plan?'**

Other great questions we would ask are:

> **'What are the effects of not taking this action?'**
>
> **'What could stop you from doing this?'**
>
> **'What needs to happen for you to do this?'**

These questions build in strength to the goal and solidity to the plan. These are the key questions that, when asked with respect and an air of expectation, will see your coachee moving forwards even when circumstances back at home and work are busy. These questions will prepare her for progress even amidst hectic schedules and unexpected problems.

Make sure you understand each section of the TGROW model and practice, practice, practice. Even qualified, experienced coaches still need to remember to trust it. Keep with it and mould it to fit each of your female coachees to get the best from them.

Now you understand the TGROW model, combine that with what you've learnt so far and bear the following points in mind.

The Goal

You will need to understand and ask how her goal relates to the rest of her life and the people she cares about. We've already heard how important it is to a woman that those she cares about are OK – if her goal is likely to have a negative impact on any of those around her, she will need to have an incredibly strong reason for carrying it out. In other words, she needs to buy into the goal not only in terms of her own dreams and aspirations but what is best for everyone else too. As coaches, we are only human; we naturally want the best for our coachees, so to hear a woman tell her most secret desires in one breath and then have her explain them away, diminish them or to put them in second place for the sake of others, can be frustrating. Wouldn't you instinctively want to stand up for those dreams? Or remind her that it is her life and that she is allowed to put herself first for once? But it's not your life, so she doesn't need someone else telling her what to do, being her supporter or campaigning on her behalf. She needs to be taken seriously, to be validated and her goal needs to be in line with what she believes is right; that is your job. You must ensure that your coachee understands the relationship she has between her own goals and the significant people in her life. When she has arrived at a goal that takes all viewpoints into account, she'll buy into it and she'll stick with it.

The Reality

We've warned you about not getting too caught up in reality but, coach, do let your coachee talk. Don't rush her through it or she won't have time to express her emotional response to what is happening to her. If her goal is about 'clarity' or 'understanding' she may need more time in this part of the model to investigate her emotions. Your job is to move her to a position of empowerment, not hustle her to the end, so listen to her, hear every word, acknowledge her emotionally and then when you move on, she will come with you. Her decisions will be rooted in a firm understanding.

The Options

Keep plugging for more options. You would do this while coaching a man too, of course, but the trick here is to plug for options using her most natural gift – visualisation. Ask for images, ask what she sees, ask what her intuition is telling her, then check her emotional response to her options and how these fit with her family and those around her. Don't pin her down to agreeing to any one option at this time. Keep the suggestions coming – ask her to be creative, to look into the future, to work backwards in her mind. Her mind is flexible, quick and able; this is the time to capitalise on that.

The Will

Remember to watch your intonation all the way through this section. Ask why would she do this? What is it that will make this plan work over every other she has tried? What benefit will this have on her and everyone involved? How will it work with her values and ethics? The female brain is wired for win-wins. If she wins, someone else has to win too – that's the deal. Find out how everyone else wins and you will compound her decision. This is one of the most influential conversations your coachee could have and it is how women thrive – it is how to coach a woman.

4 Question Etiquette: How to Cut Through a Woman's Mind Mist With Questions

To turn yourself into a coach of excellence you need to understand how to ask some of the simplest yet most powerful questions. A key talent of an expert coach for women is asking questions that will tap into the coachee's mind in a way which none of her friends, family or colleagues have been trained to do. The right questions can change the way your coachee thinks and unlock insights which are potentially life changing.

In this chapter we will be teaching you how to build your expertise by highlighting questions that promote communication, talking, discussion – a skill deeply rooted in Key Principle 6 (women learn best through discussion and have highly developed verbal skills).

You will understand by now that the TGROW model forms the basic structure of a coaching session. Think of that model acting rather like the trellis up against a garden wall. If the TGROW model is the trellis, then the questions are the vines that weave in and around it. No matter how sturdy your trellis, if your vine isn't strong enough or healthy enough to climb around it, to interweave and grow in different directions, it will never find its way to the top of the trellis, where it wants to be. For the vine to be healthy and strong, it doesn't just need to grow directly upwards, it needs to move confidently and explore every inch of the trellis so it understands how to stick to it and how to use it as a support tool for getting to the top. It is in this creative movement around the trellis that it develops the strength, structure and depth it needs to grow year after year. When you are coaching a woman confidently, using the TGROW model and weaving your questions around it, the coachee's learning and exploration is your way of making sure that the answers she comes to are her own and that those answers make sense to her, so she is able to run with them and make them fit her life in a way that no other discussion could.

The kind of questions you ask, the intonation you use and the manner in which those questions follow on from each other will form an integral part of your coaching session. The questions should promote discussion, inspire thought, build in forward thinking and enable your female coachee to access parts of her mind she has long since forgotten about. Her answers are there; the questions you ask will mean she will access them much more easily. Your questions will respectfully dig, probe and remove blockages. They will be respectfully firm and you won't let your coachee off the hook with sweeping statements or glossed over generalisations. This is where you will be of most help to your female coachee. Asking her the same questions her friends and family might ask will only do so much. Your skill in asking the right questions at the right time will mean that your coachee gets to dig deeper into the topics and goals she discusses with you – it will get her thinking about her own behaviour and her own reactions to events. Your questions will encourage her to find solutions that will fit her and only her. On occasion your questions might be challenging or tough (although asked respectfully), but equally it is often the most obvious questions that significantly impact our coachees. Questions such as:

▌ **'How does that work for you?'**

or

▌ **'When is that OK with you?'**

have often caused our coachees to take a closer look at what is acceptable for them, what they are putting up with and where their boundaries are. So you see how important understanding the power of your questions is and how developing your questioning technique can either make or break a coaching session with a woman.

If you are already a coach, asking questions will be second nature to you. You will already understand the value of using open, probing and enquiring questions that promote discussion, solutions and movement forwards. You will have learned how imperative it is that you have no input into the end result of the coaching session and no 'best solution' for your coachee stored in your head ready to present when she is having difficulty accessing her own wisdom.

Traditional coaching books are likely to clarify open and closed questions, leading questions, scenario building questions, forward projecting questions, how and when to use 'why', and so will we, but we think using questions in a coaching session with a woman should be taken one step further. We believe that it is necessary to skilfully encompass our six key principles with your questions and understand question etiquette. In our opinion, for anyone to call themselves an expert in this niche area of coaching, this is vital and here is the reason.

Research has shown that women are much more likely to analyse their own behaviour (remember Key Principle 6 – women are more self critical). As football coach Anson Dorrance comments: 'If you make a general criticism of a men's team, they all think you are talking about someone else ... If you make a general criticism of women every woman in the room thinks you are talking about her' (Dorrance, 2005).

If a man knows he is good at something, he will accept that head on and asking him questions about his area of expertise or his qualifications won't shake his confidence or his ego. Ask a woman the same questions though with the wrong inference and she will take it to heart. You will have her questioning her behaviour and values and wondering how valid her thought process was in the first place. At best you will dull her ability to trust in her own answers and at worst you will leave her questioning her behaviour, personality and previously trusted approach to everyday situations. A man is more likely to approach your question in a matter of fact manner and is much less likely to turn it back on himself as an individual. You can completely ruin a coaching session with a woman by asking: 'How could that work?' in a tone that says, 'Mmm ... let's be honest now, that's never going to work in a month of Sundays is it?' So you can see the need to bear in mind question etiquette when coaching your female coachees if you are to ask valid, respectful and effective questions during your session.

For us, question etiquette is about responding to six basic rules:

1 **Respect your coachee's answer.** If she closes a door after you've asked a question, respect that closure and take your line of questioning down a different path – one she gives you permission to go down.

2 **Challenge her thought process.** If she is contradicting herself it will help to point that out; if she is going round in circles and playing with the same options and none of them are sticking, point that out to her; if she is making sweeping

statements help her to be specific by asking and clarifying exactly what she means.

3 **Choose your tone carefully and your thought processes even more carefully.** Let's be clear here – your female coachee has a built-in x-ray right into your thought processes. If you don't believe she can do something, your tone and what is running through your mind will be as visible to her as a flashing neon light above your head!

4 **Never presume.** Never presume you know what your coachee means. Women don't like this one little bit! We've both seen demonstration coaching sessions by our students, and also by some professionals, where they've presumed their female coachee means one thing and they've been told in no uncertain terms that they meant something entirely different.

5 **Keep your questions simple.** You will be coaching intelligent, articulate women but if you complicate your question with sub-clauses or go round in circles when you ask it, she will get lost trying to understand what you are asking. Your questions need to reflect that you already know she will be fixing more than one issue at a time in her mind. If she is spending valuable energy trying to decipher your questions or getting confused as to which part to answer first, you will cloud her clear thinking and hinder her multilevel approach.

6 **Don't let your coachee feel she is being interrogated.** Your coachee wants space to explore her thoughts; she doesn't want to feel as though she is at a job interview. When you start coaching it is easy to focus so much on your questioning skills that you forget that coaching is a conversation, not a direct fire of questions.

Let's explore these basic rules in a bit more detail.

1 Respect her answer

It is in a woman's nature to tell her coach the whole situation she finds herself in. It is during this process that enquiring questions such as:

▎ **'Tell me more about that?'**

and

▌ 'How does this situation impact on other areas of your life?'

will encourage her to talk. Consequently she is likely to mention other people and other issues, giving you background and depth to her topic and goal. There will undoubtedly be aspects of her story that she doesn't feel are relevant to explore during the session, and while it is your job to probe and ask questions, it is not your job to encourage her to look at something that *you* feel is important if your coachee doesn't agree. Here's what we mean.

Coachee's Topic – to talk about the disharmony currently running through her team at work

Coachee's Goal – to come up with a different approach for dealing with Susan, her most dominating team member

COACH: So tell me more about Susan?

COACHEE: Ah well, she's taking over the team really. I'm in charge actually, and while my team know that, she's starting to influence them, so that they ask her for direction and clarification instead of me. It's been getting worse for months now and they've started to ask her whether they can have days off instead of me! She's really undermining my authority ... *(pause)* I've noticed that Emma (the most junior of the team) in particular has started to look up to her and I don't want her copying her behaviour. In fact she has her own set of issues – she's constantly late and doesn't check her work properly – so I want her to be inspired by someone I'd consider to be a responsible role model and Susan really isn't that person! Actually, Emma is another issue entirely and I'm not sure yet how to deal with that situation.

COACH: It sounds like both those ladies come with their own issues.

COACHEE: Yes, Emma drives me mad actually!

COACH: We started off the session talking about a strategy for dealing with Susan, your most dominating team member, but it also sounds like Emma is causing you a lot of tension too – is our initial goal of talking about Susan still appropriate?

COACHEE: Yes, I think so – she's my priority at the moment. Emma I can deal with – she's infuriating and I don't yet know how to tackle her, but I'm confident I can, so yes, Susan is still my priority.

COACH: OK.

The coach has identified that Emma is causing her coachee some anxiety as well as Susan and so checks if Susan is still the priority for the session. The coachee says yes she is and so the coach accepts that and continues with the session and the initial goal. After all, who is the coach (who may never have met either Susan or Emma) to suggest which of her two team members she should deal with first? Remember, it is not the coach's job to assume that Emma should be dealt with first and end up leading the coachee to that end. We've highlighted below how *not* to approach this by giving you a different ending to that same scenario:

COACH: We started off the session talking about a strategy for dealing with Susan, your most dominating team member, but it also sounds like Emma is causing you a lot of tension too – is our initial goal of talking about Susan still appropriate?

COACHEE: Yes, I think so – she's my priority at the moment. Emma I can deal with – she's infuriating and I don't yet know how to tackle her, but I'm confident I can, so yes, Susan is still my priority.

COACH: Would it not seem sensible to deal with the person you feel most confident about?

COACHEE: No, I don't think so. Emma isn't the real cause of the unrest in the team. She infuriates everyone to some extent but it's Susan who is causing most of the unrest.

COACH: Well, sometimes if you sort out some of the smaller issues, the bigger problems, such as Susan, get easier to deal with. Have you ever found that?

COACHEE: No, for me, I always deal with the difficult problems first and leave the smaller ones – but in fact, it's not Emma who is causing the problems, it's Susan and I honestly feel like I need to focus on her! *(said with irritation)*

This scenario makes for much more uncomfortable reading. In the coaching space the coachee understands her situation the best; the coach is there to facilitate clearer thought processes in a way that makes sense to the coachee. This example is not only ineffective but utterly destroys the coaching relationship. The coachee is now irritated with the coach. The coach has pushed her own personal way of dealing with big issues first onto the coachee in a very 'I know how to sort this situation for you' type of way and it goes against every single ethical coaching grain there is.

In this situation the coachee is clearly strong – she knows her own mind and won't be swayed – but how different could that situation have been if the coachee wasn't as sure of herself.

> COACH: We started off the session talking about a strategy for dealing with Susan, your most dominating team member, but it also sounds like Emma is causing you a lot of tension too – is our initial goal of talking about Susan still appropriate?
>
> COACHEE: Yes, I think so – she's my priority at the moment. Emma I can deal with – she's infuriating and I don't yet know how to tackle her, but I'm confident I can, so yes, Susan is still my priority.
>
> COACH: Would it not seem sensible to deal with the person you feel most confident about?
>
> COACHEE: Oh ... do you think?
>
> COACH: Well, sometimes if you sort out some of the smaller issues, the bigger problems, such as Susan, get easier to deal with. Have you ever found that?
>
> COACHEE: Um, well yes sometimes. To be honest I know I'm not handling any of this very well. I'm happy to take any advice you have – you're the expert.

Now it seems the coaching session has moved to more of a mentoring session. What is more, the coachee is losing confidence that she has been dealing with 'any' of this very well and she has completely lost where her sense of self was telling her to start – that is with Susan. This is dangerous ground and not one a coach should find herself in. Some of the language the coachee uses at this juncture is also a giveaway – 'advice', 'expert'. The coach is not an expert in the coachee's situation and this coach has undermined our coachee's confidence with just two leading questions. We will talk about leading questions below but we hope that you can see how important it is to respect your coachee's answer – respect the fact that she knows instinctively which way is best for her and respect that it is likely to be different from yours.

2 Challenge her thought process

There is nothing more helpful than having another person really listen to what we are saying. That means noticing the language we use and the number of times we might repeat certain things. It is helpful for a woman to find her coaching sessions challenging; when she does, and when she finds answers that make sense to her, it is because she has been prompted to think a little further into her usual thought processes. Here's what we mean by respectfully challenging her thought processes:

COACHEE: Well, as I was saying, everything Susan does at the minute seems to annoy me.

COACH: Everything?

COACHEE: Absolutely. From the moment she walks in, I think 'Oh here we go again!' She'll find more ways to directly undermine me and more ways to make decisions without my knowledge or consent – keeping track of her is virtually impossible. She does everything just within the bounds of reasonable, yet she undermines my authority every time.

COACH: What I'm hearing is that you feel everything she does is a direct threat to your authority, is that right?

COACHEE: Well, probably not everything. You know when she does her job, she's very effective at it – and actually when my back is against the wall, in a meeting or something, she has stood up for decisions I've made. It's just that sometimes I don't think she believes I'm making the right decisions and I think that's when she tends to take over.

COACH: Tell me more about the times when you feel she takes over?

The coach challenged our coachee's thinking here and she did so because she had picked up on her language. The coachee used 'everything' a lot and when the coach brought that to her attention by clarifying that she was hearing correctly, the coachee rephrased that to 'sometimes', which then led on to more information about Susan's behaviour and how the coachee might be able to deal with it differently. Note here that the coach is not trying to get the coachee to see that the word 'everything' is incorrect or a sweeping statement, she's just challenging it.

Here is an example of how the coaching session might have gone differently:

COACHEE: Well, as I was saying, everything Susan does at the minute seems to annoy me.

COACH: Everything?

COACHEE: Absolutely. From the moment she walks in, I think 'Oh here we go again!' She'll find more ways to directly undermine me and more ways to make decisions without my knowledge or consent – keeping track of her is virtually impossible. She does everything just within the bounds of reasonable, yet she undermines my authority every time.

COACH: What I'm hearing is that you feel everything she does is a direct threat to your authority, is that right?

COACHEE: Yes, I believe it is. It's just something about the way she looks at me or the sideways smile she gives herself when someone asks her permission to do something, as opposed to asking me. She knows what she's doing. In fact, I think it stems back to last year when I got this promotion over her. I actually think she's quite determined to make me look like I can't do the job. I really need to take control of this situation now and stamp my authority on my role. I felt sorry for her not getting it – she told one or two people that she knew the job was hers and that the interview stage was just a formality – so when I got the job, we were both surprised actually. I think I've given her so much leeway because I knew she lost face. I can see now I've given her too much control.

Can you see how this session is panning out completely differently? A great example of how challenging your coachee could prove to reveal valuable insights into the situation. Challenging without leading and without coming across as the expert, that's the key.

3 Choose your tone carefully

In our experience, women pick up on undercurrents much more quickly than our male counterparts. As Moir and Jessel point out: 'Even before they can understand language, girls seem to be better than boys at identifying the emotional content of speech' (1998: 35). This is an ability which they attribute to 'the basic difference in the newborn brain ... the superior male efficiency in spatial ability, the greater female skill in speech' (1998: 56).

Women can sniff out intention, atmosphere, ulterior motives and quick eye movements that can tell a thousand stories in a millisecond. Moir and Jessel suggest that women's 'superiority in many of the senses can be clinically measured ... it is what counts for women's almost supernatural intuition. Women are simply better equipped to notice things to which men are comparatively blind ... women are better at ... picking up social cues, picking up important nuances of meaning from tones of voice or intensity of expression' (1998: 19). They suggest that from infancy girls show the greater interest in communicating with people and this bias towards the personal shows up in experiments. In a test in which a group of children are shown pictures of people and objects through binocular type lenses, Moir and Jessel report that 'the boys reported seeing significantly more things than people and the girls more people than things' (1998: 56). They infer from such experiments that 'Women tend to be better judges of character ... and have a greater sensitivity to other people's preferences' (1998: 19).

The point is that women pick up on disappointment no matter what someone is saying. We pick up on disapproval and subliminal thoughts without a word being uttered, and we do this very easily and very naturally: 'females are equipped to receive a greater range of sensory information ... to place a primacy on personal relationships and to communicate' (1998: 17).

If in a coaching session your question says 'I trust you know the answer' but your eyes say 'No chance – you're completely lost!' your female coachee *will* know! If your mouth is asking 'How will that work?' and your tone says 'You know that doesn't stand a chance of working don't you?' she will see through you. If your question clarifies 'So, you want to be a manager' but your eyes say 'You've got *so* much to learn before *that* happens' you will lose her trust in an instant. Only an excellent coach can honestly say they are free of limiting beliefs, that they know their coachees are capable of achieving and can genuinely put their preferred outcome to one side. But this only comes to those who understand that their tone and thought processes are see-through to their female coachees. It is everyday human behaviour to put our own spin on other people's dreams and aspirations. There is no getting away from it, and coaches are not faultless, but during that very precious coaching space, for that hour or two, they are able to do so. It is the gift of being able to coach a woman.

4 Never presume

No one really knows what is going on in someone else's mind. Even married couples and long term partners get taken aback by what their other halves think about certain topics if they ask, so why should a coach presume to know how their coachee will think, react or act? It is true that our coachees tell us lots of information about themselves. It is also true that some coach–coachee relationships span months and sometimes years, so we do come to a point where we build up history with coachees, but that still doesn't give us licence to assume that we know what they are thinking. Here's an example of a coach who knows never to presume:

> COACHEE: Susan's behaviour really seems to affect me most when the others go to her for direction.
>
> COACH: What is it about that which particularly affects you?
>
> COACHEE: I've always prided myself on being able to communicate very well, by getting people to value their role within the team, and I suppose I feel as though they don't think I'm good at communication if they're running to Susan every five minutes.
>
> COACH: What does communication mean to you?

Now here's an example of a coach who presumes to know her coachee:

> COACHEE: Susan's behaviour really seems to affect me most when the others go to her for direction.
>
> COACH: How is being able to direct others important?
>
> COACHEE: Being able to direct people isn't important ... I actually think it's the ability to be able to communicate where you see your team

heading. That's the important thing here – and she isn't party to some of the discussions I have with my boss and how he needs the team to shape up in the long term.

There is a little tension here between the coach and the coachee but technically that isn't a bad question – after all it is open, enquiring and information promoting. What makes it a poor question is that the coach has made up her mind about what is important to the coachee whereas in the first example the coach says, 'What is it about that which particularly affects you?'

Here is when that question would have been entirely appropriate:

COACHEE: Susan's behaviour really seems to affect me most when the others go to her for direction. Giving direction, to my mind, should only come from the person in charge, and it's not just what direction is being given but how that direction is given.

COACH: How is being able to direct others important?

COACHEE: It's about working with a team's strengths, about promoting the good aspects of one personality and the good aspects of another personality. It's blending the two, and Susan just doesn't get that.

That sounds much better doesn't it? The coach is listening to her coachee all the way – in the previous example she really hasn't listened properly and it has got her into trouble. Later we have a whole chapter on honing your listening skills, but we can't emphasise enough at this juncture that all of these skills, put together, are what makes coaching a woman work seamlessly and beautifully. Presuming you know what she means, thinks or is going to say next will put up a big brick wall between the two of you. Practise in your everyday life. Ask your female counterparts what they mean, what they think, how they would react, what their initial thoughts are – ask more and you will be surprised what you hear.

5 Keep your questions simple

Sometimes the coach's thoughts can run faster than the coachee's answers, so the coach wants to ask several things at the same time or add explanations and elaborations to the questions. For example, if your coachee's topic is about changing her job, asking

> **'If you think about what makes you want to change your job, what are your reasons? And what does that tell you about your attitude to work and what your criteria for deciding where to work will be?'**

will leave her worn out before she even begins to try to answer. What is more, she will have forgotten the last part of the question before she finishes answering. It is an impossible question to answer properly and thoughtfully. Keep your questions simple, even if you have to write down the odd note on your sheet of paper as a cue for you to ask another question in the next few minutes.

A simple

> **'What is important to you about where you work?'**

will be much more helpful – your coachee's answers will be clearer and if you leave space for her to hear her own thoughts and enough room for her multilevel thinking to move in and around her mind, you will be giving her something her friends, family and colleagues won't – time to think, time to consider and time to evaluate.

6 Don't interrogate your coachee

If your coachee wants a session to talk about changing her job, you need to remember that you will be having a conversation with her – it is not an interview. Coaching is all about conversing with your coachee in a way that brings about clarity, solutions and positivity, so beware not to fire one question after another at her.

This is an example of how not to do it:

COACH: Where do you work?

COACHEE: I'm an office manager for a firm of solicitors.

COACH:	How long have you worked for this firm of solicitors?
COACHEE:	Six years.
COACH:	When would you want to leave the firm?
COACHEE:	I'm not sure.
COACH:	What else have you thought of doing?
COACHEE:	Possibly training as a teacher.
COACH:	Any other options?
COACHEE:	No.
COACH:	Who have you spoken to about giving up your job?
COACHEE:	Just my sister.

An hour of being questioned like that would give you both a headache and won't have achieved much for the coachee. Not only that but it will put your female coachee in a position of feeling as though you have the answers and she is being interrogated so you can give her a prescription. We already know by now that is not the approach of an excellent coach, so here is a much better way for the conversation to run:

COACH:	Tell me more about your current work.
COACHEE:	I've been working as an office manager in a firm of solicitors for about six years and to be honest I'd like a change. The job's OK and I earn a good salary but I'd like to feel that I'm doing something more worthwhile with my life. At the moment, every day is the same, dealing with people phoning to complain about their solicitor and listening to the solicitors moaning about everything, even their morning coffees.
COACH:	So am I right in thinking that you're quite happy with what you're earning but you would like a change and you particularly want to do something that you feel is more worthwhile, in a more positive atmosphere?
COACHEE:	Yes that's right. I've been wondering about teaching. Teachers probably moan as well but I'd feel really pleased if I'd made a difference in a child's life.

In this short conversation, the coach has already gleaned much more information from her coachee. By summarising and reflecting back to your coachee what you think she is telling you, instead of firing off a series of questions, you give her the chance to hear what she has been thinking, spoken out loud by someone else, probably for the first time.

If you think of coaching as a series of questions, you put yourself under immense pressure to come up with a non-stop stream of inspiration and you risk turning the session into an unpleasant cross-examination. If you combine open questions with some reflecting back and summarising you get a smooth flowing conversation in which your coachee can concentrate on her thoughts and answers.

One question our students often ask is, 'Do I need to know a lot about what my coachee wants to talk about?' They worry that they should be experts in just about every topic their future coachees might bring to them. That is an impossible task and completely unnecessary. In fact we find that *not* understanding the work our coachees do or the situations they are in means that we ask those really naive questions that no one else thinks to ask. When a coachee has to explain to her coach from scratch those things that she has taken for granted up till now she will often start to see the situation differently. That perspective will be invaluable.

So now you understand question etiquette, let's look at the questions themselves in a bit more detail. You will need to become familiar with the following:

- open and closed questions
- clarifying questions
- leading questions
- scenario building questions
- forward projecting questions
- how and when to use 'why'

Open and closed questions

The basic difference between open and closed questions is that closed questions give rise to yes/no answers and open questions give rise to discussion, information, learning and exploration. Typical closed questions start with 'Could ...', 'Would ...', 'Does ...', 'Should ...', 'Are ...' and 'Do ...' They all lend themselves to mostly yes/no answers which can leave the coach doing all the work and the coachee not giving away anything and not feeling the need to talk or explore their situation. When we teach the first stage of questions to our students, our emphasis is on practising conversations with no closed questions in them at all. Practise at home or at work yourself – try asking what you want but just using open questions.

Open questions typically start with words like 'What ...', 'How ...', 'Tell me ...', 'When ...', 'Where ...' and 'What ...' These questions are really difficult to put yes/no answers to so your coachees will tell you more – it is as simple as that. And when they tell you more, they are hearing about what *they* think, feel or want from their situations. It is learning for both the coach and coachee.

Open questions can also break through negativity. Imagine this: your coachee says she wants a pay rise. If you asked

> ▍ **'Can you ask your boss for a rise?'**

she could of course answer simply yes or no but if she's already thinking to herself 'I can't really ask for a rise in this economic climate,' then her answer to you will automatically be no.

If however, you ask an open question such as:

> ▍ **'What can you do about getting the pay rise you want?'**

you've opened her mind to the possibility that there *is* something she can do.

Clarifying questions

We teach our students the importance of clarifying what their coachees mean very early on in their training – it is such an important aspect of the coaching session. We've touched on this already and so what you might have noticed is that clarifying questions are often closed questions. So how does that work if we've just told you that closed questions are poor coaching questions? Intonation is everything. Here's what we mean:

> **'Do you mean that while Emma isn't a good team member that your priority is with dealing with Susan first?'**

If that sentence was said with interest, in an enquiring fashion and in a way that gives your coachee the opportunity to disagree, it is an excellent clarification question. Where questions are closed, the attitude of those questions should be open – that is the difference.

When our students have had at least a month of using many more open questions than they would previously have done, we introduce the concept of using the odd closed question in appropriate circumstances, with the correct intonation and in a suitable place. One case study we remember very clearly was when a student started the coaching session brilliantly. She used the T and the G of TGROW very well, we got to the R and that went well, then during O (where your coachee should be exploring all the possible options) she used a series of closed questions, literally one after the other. The closed questions meant the coachee and the coach both got stuck. We were able to pinpoint exactly which stage the student was at when the session started to go downhill – a valuable lesson for the coach and a great learning curve. So don't forget: clarifying is vital, necessary and hugely valuable but open questions are insightful, accessing and solution focused. Learn to take notice of which questions you naturally gravitate towards in everyday life and you will become a more aware communicator both in and out of the coaching environment.

Leading questions

Leading questions are those that insinuate a route has already been mapped out by the coach. Leading questions are exactly that; a poorly trained coach will try to lead their coachee, insisting they know where their answers lie. Leading questions are more difficult to spot – they can be open or closed – but intonation is always a giveaway, as is facial expression and body language. However, a good coach can spot when they are leading by how they feel when they ask a question. Leading questions only happen when a coach has something on their mind – a place where they want the coachee to get to, something they want the coachee to see – so that unsettled, anxious, frustrated feeling will be the most apparent giveaway to the coach.

Here's a way of remembering why leading questions aren't good for your coachee:

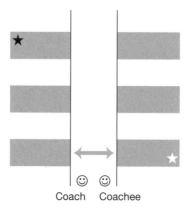

Coach   Coachee

Imagine this is a hotel corridor and the grey rectangles are rooms on either side of the corridor. Coach and coachee are looking to find a prize for the coachee which is hidden in one of the rooms. The white star is the prize the coach is convinced the coachee is looking for. The black star is actually the prize that the coachee is going to find most helpful. As the coach and the coachee walk to the first set of doors, the coachee has an option. Which door will she take? If the coach is convinced they need to take the right hand door they could find themselves asking leading questions such as:

> **'What do you think you might find behind the right hand door?'**
>
> **'Do you think you'd be more productive opening the right hand door?'**

Their mind will be so consumed that they are convinced they are right, such that they won't give the coachee the opportunity to consider how many more options might be available to them.

Good questions at this juncture might be:

> **'Which door would you like to open first?'**
>
> **'Look down the whole corridor at all of the doors – are there any that catch your eye in particular?'**
>
> **'Where you do you think would be the best place to start?'**

These questions give the coachee licence to start wherever they feel, to make decisions without interference, and that is perfect because you are encouraging their learning.

When we explained this to one of our coaching students, one of them said 'but when coaching is meant to help people find their answers sooner rather than later – and you know where their answer is – isn't it wrong to keep it from them?' The point is you don't know where their answers are stored! You might know where *your* answer is stored, but you only know that because of every experience you've ever been through, because of every conversation you've ever had, because you remember when you did something well or when you made mistakes. You only know where your answer is because you learnt it along the way. So firstly, why would you deny someone else that same learning curve and secondly, your perfect answer is virtually guaranteed to be different from theirs.

Now consider the model below. This is where the coach has let the coachee open doors, wander in and out of the hotel rooms, and pick up information and learning from each room along the way:

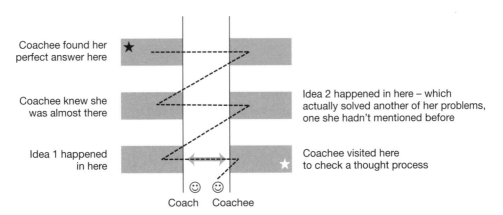

In this scenario, the coachee has visited the rooms she considered intuitively necessary at the time. A learning point or an idea happened in each one, which eventually led to her finding the right prize for her. Without that toing and froing, the learning curve and thought process may never have happened and the coachee may never have found her ideal prize. Not only that, have you noticed what the coachee found in the right hand middle room? An answer to a problem she hadn't mentioned up until now. This is typical of a female coachee and follows Key Principle 3 – women have the ability to fix several problems at the same time, even when they are only talking to you about one issue. This happens more frequently in coaching sessions than you might imagine, according to Neil Carlson and William Buskist: 'Women think on multiple levels when they have a conversation, possibly because the tract of fibres which connects the two halves of the brain is larger in women, making simultaneous activity on both sides of the brain more likely' (1996: 472).

We all know that women are famous for multitasking and this is no different. Just because a coaching session creates a space to focus doesn't mean that the multitasking part of her brain won't kick in – it is when it is most active. If the coach tries to push their coachee straight to a specific answer there is no room for that powerful, creative and magical thinking to happen. Your female coachee will leave the session feeling not entirely listened to, not completely convinced of her plan and still questioning how she will fit it into her life.

Scenario building questions

Scenario based questions tap beautifully into Key Principle 5 – women are able to use visualisation very effectively. These questions give women the chance to test possible solutions. Here's what we mean:

> COACHEE: If I changed the office around and put the desks in a different position, I think it would make a real difference to how the team works.

> COACH: OK, let's imagine that you've done that – all the desks are exactly where you want them and it's made a tangible difference to how the team works. Where would you have put everyone?

> COACHEE: Well, I'd be in the middle I think – with all my team around me – that way I'd feel like I could see what everyone was doing and feel on top of the situation. I'd also be in close contact to everyone. At the moment, my desk is in the far right corner, so for instance Emma is three desk spaces away from me. It's no wonder I suppose she asks Susan for direction – Susan is literally the next desk to her.

In this scenario, the coachee is able to visualise not only what she would do but how it might impact her team. The coachee clearly thinks this is a good idea. But she may not have done – the session could have gone like this:

COACHEE: If I changed the office around and put the desks in a different position, I think it would make a real difference to how the team works.

COACH: OK, let's imagine that you've done that – all the desks are exactly where you want them and it's made a tangible difference to how the team works. Where would you have put everyone?

COACHEE: Well, I'd be in the middle I think – with all my team around me – that way I'd feel like I could see what everyone was doing and feel on top of the situation. But having said that – I don't want them to feel like I'm spying on them. I might look like I'm desperate to be in control and that is definitely not the look I'm after!

COACH: OK. Imagine you altered the desks around and you got the exact 'look' you were after. How would they be arranged then?

COACHEE: ... *(pause)* If I look at everyone's weaknesses that might help: Emma for instance stares out of the window – I hate that. I think we'll have Emma in the centre of the room. Shirley's like a yo-yo sometimes, up and down to the toilet. I don't mind but when she passes everyone's desk it can be annoying and disruptive, so I think I'll put her near the door. And I think I'll move Susan away from Emma. Yes that'll work, I'll go between Susan and Emma, then I can keep Emma on the straight and narrow very well.

Another great question for scenario building comes from fellow coach for women and author of *Mothers Work!*, Jessica Chivers. Here's what she says on her website (www.jessicachivers.com):

In my coaching work with professional women I've noticed that where there's a confidence or self-belief issue – for example women who've excelled in their field and now want to put those skills to work on a self-employment basis or small business basis – women can be 'unlocked' by a simple question about how or what they'd advise a friend to think, feel or do. I can't imagine suggesting that a male coachee would feel comfortable being asked what his best mate would do! I think that's a coaching technique especially useful for women. I had a coachee, let's call her Harriet, who worked for local government and from what I can gather is very well-respected and good at what she does. She always seemed thoughtful, articulate and very self-aware, yet when it came to seeing how she could make self-employment work and bring the money home she lacked the belief in her skills and talents. Asking her to think about what she'd advise her best friend to do if she were in this position and asking her to tell me what her colleagues would say if they could hear her talking in a downbeat way about herself, lifted her to a new place.

Forward projecting questions

Forward projecting questions give your female coachees the opportunity to access solutions they haven't already thought of and also work with Key Principle 5, their natural ability to be able to visualise. Let's imagine that your coachee is completely stuck, they don't know what their next move should be and they are really not sure how to tackle a situation. Asking them to view that situation from their place of 'stuckness' to a place of choice can be difficult. Instead, try asking them to look at it from a point in time where they've already made perfect solutions and you will get different answers. Use questions such as:

> **'If we were meeting here precisely a year from today and you'd got this situation completely sorted and were very happy with the outcome, what would have happened?'**
>
> **'Imagine that you handled this perfectly and you were telling someone what you did – what would you be saying?'**

Looking at a problem from a different perspective is part of what coaching is all about, as these questions illustrate. As Dina Glouberman says in her book *Life Choices and Life Changes through Image Work*, 'to resolve a problem, or to find a way through a difficulty, or to make an important choice you need to vary your perspective and approaches as much as possible' (1989: 313).

Forward thinking questions are also a great safeguard for trainee or new coaches if they feel they've lost their way at any point during the session. If the coach loses their train of thought (which does happen) or if questions aren't coming naturally, any question based in a forward thinking direction will give the session a solid base to proceed from with confidence.

How and when to use 'why'

'Why' questions need to be handled with care. Think kid gloves, think delicate laundry cycle, think antique glass heirloom. Why can be such a judgemental question. Some of the best business people we've ever coached are terrified by questions that start with why. Ask someone why and you are generally asking them to back up their reasoning for why they did or didn't do something. You are asking for results and reasons – it is not generally a comfortable word to be asked. Yes, the job of a coach is to challenge their coachees, but that is our point – 'challenge' not 'scare off'! Instead of using the word why to ask a question, practise asking it another way – using open questions, for example. If you look hard enough you will find an equivalent question that is far more appropriate and doesn't back your coachee into a corner of having to explain herself to you. Consider these questions:

> **(Wrong)** **Why do you do that?**
>
> **(Right)** **What is it about doing it that way that makes sense to you?**
>
> **(Wrong)** **Why don't you tell her off?**
>
> **(Right)** **How could you challenge her behaviour?**
>
> **(Wrong)** **Why do you think that didn't work?**
>
> **(Right)** **What was it specifically that didn't work?**
>
> **(Wrong)** **Why did you choose that strategy?**
>
> **(Right)** **What made that strategy particularly appealing to you?**

You can see how these questions really say the same thing but in judgemental and non-judgemental ways. You will get far more information, cooperation and forward thinking strategies from your coachee from using the latter in each case.

There is just one scenario where a why question works very nicely and that is at the end of a session. Think back to Chapter 3 on TGROW where why can give your coachee emotional buy-in. Here's how to use why successfully:

COACH: So ... you've got a great plan by the sounds of it – are you happy?

COACHEE: Yes very!

COACH: How will you integrate your plan when you get back into your routine?

COACHEE: Well, I think my routine is going to have to change a bit. I'll do it though ... I'm determined.

COACH: OK, so tell me this. Imagine you've had a really bad day at work ... you're hungry, tired and have plenty of other things to do instead of running around the block as you've planned today. Why would you still do it?

COACHEE: Why?

COACH: Yes! Why on earth would you? *(smiling)*

COACHEE: *(laughs)* Good question! Actually I'm really going to need to think about that. I know that exercising in the evening would be a great way to wind down but I think I might need more than that if my day's been *that* bad. *(Pause)* I'd have to have a push ... something to remind me why I'm doing it I think. I might also forget too until it's really in my routine. OK, what I'm going to do is put a picture of a woman running on my wardrobe door. When I come in from work, whatever happens, I go upstairs, put my work clothes in the laundry basket and find something more comfortable to wear. If I have a photo there, it'll remind me to put on my jogging bottoms and t-shirt, not my jeans. The picture will also need to be of a really fit person running, so it'll remind me I'm not as fit as them yet! That'll work.

Can you see how the why question here is helpful and not threatening? The reason this why question works is because the coach is genuinely interested in the coachee's own motivation behind her plan. If you're honestly wondering *if* and *why* a coachee will stick to their plan, it is OK to ask – in a respectful fashion with a tone that encourages them to find an answer that will work. Do that and you will be your coachee's secret to real success.

What if you don't know what to ask next?

We've noticed that when our students start to practise their coaching skills they sometimes panic that their minds will go blank and they will be sitting opposite a coachee with their mouths open and nothing coming out.

This doesn't happen to a new coach as often as you might expect. If you are really listening to your coachee and getting involved in her story, you will be so curious that the next question will appear in your mind. But if it doesn't, remember that coaching is a conversation not an interview. It is fine to recap on what your coachee wanted from the session or what she has talked about so far, and by the time you've done that you will be focused again and able to carry on.

It is also acceptable to be honest. If you've been distracted for a moment, for example, by a noise or something moving in your line of vision, then say so and ask your coachee to repeat what she just said. If you can't think what to ask next because you feel stuck or you feel that the session isn't going anywhere, then be honest here as well. Ask 'Is this still a useful discussion for you?' (closed question but you want the information). If your coachee says it is then ask, 'What has been particularly helpful to talk about so far?', which will show you the direction to follow next. If she says no and that she feels stuck as well then you can ask, 'What do you feel would be a more helpful focus for us?'

Do remember Key Principle 2, that women learn best through discussion and have highly developed verbal skills. It is important to keep your coachee talking but make sure that it is helpful. Your female coachee is predisposed to be willing and able to help you to move the session forward. Always go back to what your coachee wants to get from the session to refocus you both.

Remember that questions are invitations for your coachee to explore something she cares about, to focus her thoughts, to tap into her creativity, to find new possibilities and to move forward.

5 Listen, Clarify, Listen, Clarify: The Power of Being Heard

If we were to ask you when was the last time you really felt listened to, what would you say? It might be harder to remember than you think. Being listened to, in the real sense of the word, is not just about having a conversation. It is not about everyday dialogue or family chit-chat where family members talk over each other, finish each other's sentences and can't wait to tell you the latest gossip. We mean, when was the last time someone sat with you, stopped what they were doing, looked at you and made you feel as though you were the only person in the room – when did that last happen?

The truth is, it doesn't happen that often. We spoke to Jo Hockey, Managing Director of Colne Estates (www.colneestates.com), who finds the power of being listened to in a coaching session particularly helpful as she works for herself and on her own. She says: 'We live in a fast paced world with everyone rushing around and busy with their own problems. If and when you do find time to step back and think about what's going well or what isn't going so well, it's rarely possible to find someone who has the time to listen at the same time you're ready to talk.' Some of the questions Jo has found herself answering in her coaching sessions are: 'Am I setting too many challenges?', 'Are those challenges realistic?' and 'Am I rewarding myself properly?' Jo adds: 'I find all of those questions easier to answer when my coach is listening to me talk them over. When I can chew the fat with her and bat ideas around, I'm able to focus on what I need to do. My friends are available to me, but I don't want to have those kinds of conversations with my friends, that's not what they're there for. I want to have fun with them, not strategise!' Jo finds that by booking in a session every four to six weeks, her planned coaching sessions give her the reassurance that she will be listened to and the confidence that she will be dealing with the issues she has faced during the month. She also says that having a future session booked keeps her focused on the challenges she has set herself, knowing that she will have to tell someone if she has completed them or not.

So you can see that having a space where they are really listened to is very important for many women. You will need to learn to focus on another individual and learn how to zone every other distraction out of your mind (and view), so you're able to give that kind of validity and focus. Tamara Furey of Furey Coaching (www.fureycoaching.co.uk) says: 'The honour is to listen to a coachee talking about their lives. Listening for me actually happens visually – the rest of the world drops away, I can see nothing but the coachee (not even the chair!). Only they exist, and it is almost as if they glow in that attention. It is at these times that the deepest work is done, even if I only utter a few words of reflection or clarification. It is like nothing else, and keeps me coming back again and again to coach.'

In her book *Time to Think*, Nancy Kline says: 'listening of this calibre ignites the human mind. The quality of your attention determines the quality of other people's thinking' (1999: 33). That is exactly the kind of listening we are talking about and the kind of listening you will need to understand how to grasp if you want to become a coach of excellence. When you give someone else the very best quality of your listening, you will get back in return the very best quality of their thought processes and solutions.

Now, this book is all about the qualities it takes to coach a woman, so how important is being listened to for women really? We found out. We surveyed 100 women and asked them the following question:

Which is more important to a woman (in order of importance)?

1 Being listened to
2 Hearing advice
3 Finding new and innovative ways of doing things
4 Visualising a path forward

In response, 66% of the women said that being listened to was their top priority and 45% said that being listened to and visualising a path forwards were of most importance to them – in that order. Just 4% of women said that they preferred to hear advice.

We are not saying that men don't want to be listened to – it would be preposterous to claim that a coach who specialises in coaching men, for instance, didn't have to bother listening to them – but what we are saying is that, for a woman, the opportunity to be listened to in her entirety is so very rare, and yet so very much appreciated, that this particular skill should be rated as highly by the coach as it is by the coachee.

It is vital to both sexes that their coach is able to listen with every fibre of their being. What *is* different about listening to a woman is that you will be listening for different things.

Remember Key Principle 4 – that women are emotionally literate and willing to acknowledge, explore and express emotions. Psychology research literature suggests that there is a greater willingness among women to discuss emotion directly). When talking about how perceived gender differences influence our choice of language, Stephanie Shields, author of *Speaking From the Heart*, writes 'Men get moist eyes; women weep; men *have* emotions, women *are* emotional' (2002: 171). So it is an emotional response you will be noticing to a far greater extent if you are really listening to a woman than you would if you were listening to a man. Not only will you be listening to the factual content of your female coachee's conversation but you will need to be prepared for when she expresses a greater depth of emotion. She will connect with you much more quickly and on a much deeper level if you are prepared for her conversation and understand how to respond to her.

We've already explained that your female coachee's mind works quickly, we know that her mind is able to flit from one topic to another with great flexibility, fixing and prioritising as she goes. We've also already ascertained that understanding Key Principle 3, that women have the ability to fix several problems at the same time, even when they are only talking to you about one issue, will enhance your skills as a specialist coach for women. With those two elements in mind you will be listening to several layers of your coachee's conversation all at the same time. We've seen this time and again in our own practice, and if you don't keep up with the coachee's train of thought, you could miss vital elements of her learning curve. Ineke Buskens observes:

> It is clear that research with women can be done successfully by researchers who are willing to go beyond what seems obvious and are prepared to keep unveiling layers of meaning and experience until the moment a deeper insight is reached. (2009: 3)

This is the way your listening skills should be used to help your female coachee. Your listening skills also have to work in conjunction with your clarification skills. Both have to be top quality to ensure that neither you nor your coachee are lost, confused or caught up in a world of their own during a coaching session.

Here's an example of a coach who, while she is listening, did not blend her clarification skills with her listening ability:

> COACHEE: I just think my office needs to be more user-friendly.
>
> COACH: Tell me what needs to happen to make your office more user-friendly?
>
> COACHEE: Um ... well there are boxes everywhere. I moved office you see about five months ago, and I haven't had time to take out the files yet! I think if I *(coachee mumbles and talks to herself a bit)* ... that stuff could go there ... I'm going to give that away anyway ... that'll help actually ... I can't stand that being there ... *(coachee's voice brightens)* Yes, I think that'll do it!
>
> COACH: So you know what you're doing, yes?
>
> COACHEE: Absolutely!

Do you know what is going on? No, and neither does the coach! The coachee seems to understand her own mumbles well enough but coaching can go so much further if the coachee isn't left to mutter to herself. The coach is listening and it is clear the coachee feels better and has come to a conclusion of some sort, but the coach herself is lost! By not blending her clarification and listening skills she has missed the opportunity for the coachee to explain what she is talking about, who she is talking about and the implications of her decision – don't forget that, for a woman, that is a vital part of being listened to and really heard. Key Principle 2 – that women learn best through discussion and have highly developed verbal skills – must not be overlooked, so ask her to share her thoughts with you.

Here's how that conversation could have gone:

> COACHEE: I just think my office needs to be more user-friendly
>
> COACH: Tell me what needs to happen to make your office more user-friendly?

COACHEE: Um ... well there are boxes everywhere. I moved office you see about five months ago, and I haven't had time to take out the files yet! I think if I *(coachee mumbles and talks to herself a bit)* ... that stuff could go there ...

COACH: Tell me more about that stuff?

COACHEE: Oh, well the stuff under the desk needs to be put on the shelves – just files really. In fact, half of it I probably don't need any more. I'll get Mandy to help me sort those out actually, she's good at helping me be ruthless.

COACH: OK, so I'm hearing that there are boxes everywhere and the boxes under the desk, Mandy is going to help you sort through because you probably don't need most of them, is that right?

COACHEE: Yes, in fact, while Mandy's helping me I think it'll be the ideal time to talk to her about her home life. I know she's been struggling a bit and her work hasn't been as on the ball as it could have been. Yes ... that's what I'll do, I'll ask her to help me and get us a coffee and some of those chocolate biscuits she likes. She'll like that I think.

COACH: OK, tell me more about the rest of the boxes.

COACHEE: Right, OK, the fax machine I was going to give away anyway – it's this big machine that is of no use to me any more, as my PC has a fax facility. I thought I'd give it to my mum! She's always asking me to fax things! I can't stand tripping over it actually – it'll make my space look so much bigger. Yes *(coachee's voice brightens)* I think that'll do it. I'll be so much more relaxed without that there, I'll be so much happier bringing people into my office and my staff can have private time with me again – there's no room for them *and* all the boxes right now!

COACH: OK, so Mandy is going to help you sort through the boxes under your desk because she helps you be ruthless with files. You're also going to use that time to talk to her about her home life and get in the chocolate biscuits she likes. You're going to give the fax machine away to your mum and by doing that you think your office is going to look bigger, the knock-on effect of which will be

>that you'll feel happier inviting people into your office for private time with you, is that right?
>
>COACHEE: Just hearing that makes me feel so much more relaxed! My office will be more than user-friendly – it'll be a pleasure to work in.

Can you see how much more information the coach has got out of the coachee? By listening and clarifying, listening and clarifying, the coachee knows she is being listened to, she knows the coach is following her plans and keeping up. By recapping those plans back to her, the coach is giving the coachee the opportunity to develop the picture of how her office will look in her mind. Don't forget Key Principle 5, that women are able to visualise well. None of this happened in the first scenario and while the coachee was happy enough with her plan, we'd be willing to bet that her picture of how it would look and feel wouldn't have been as clear.

Lisa Quast, author and marketing expert from Career Woman Inc. put it perfectly on her blog in 2010 when she said, 'Listen in order to understand, not reply.' That is exactly what you are doing as a coach – listening in order to understand your coachee's perspectives. Mix that with the type of clarification we've just seen in our example and you will have a very happy woman in front of you.

We spoke to Paula Hart from HRC Group (www.hrc-group.com), who says: 'I am fortunate in that I have a mentor who actively listens to me for at least an hour a month, in bite sizes of around 20 minutes (one whole hour at a time would be wonderful). It re-energises and re-motivates me to tackle issues that can seem insuperable. It also helps improve my self worth to have someone really listen to my ideas and views. Do I feel calmer? I'm already a fairly calm person, but do I feel valued? Absolutely!'

For a woman, being listened to means being heard; being heard means being visible; being visible means being valued; and when women truly feel that what they have to offer is visible and valued, then they grow. If we don't feel valued, we don't feel visible; if we don't feel visible, we don't feel heard; and if we don't feel heard, we don't offer up our suggestions, ideas, comments and opinions – they are still there, but they are never voiced. Millions of ideas are going unheard the world over because people forget to listen to each other – they finish off sentences, they talk over each other, they 'think' they hear what the other person means, they presume to know what is best, they judge too quickly and forget that others can teach us things every day. Those millions of ideas could be contributing to professions, industries, politics, schools, colleges and family life. You have the chance to change that by honing your listening skills as a coach. By learning to increase your listening skills you are not only enabling your future coachees to be heard, but you will be learning to hear your children, friends, associates, mothers at the school gate, older people in the community. You will be giving a voice to someone possibly for the first time in their life – it is that dramatic!

When Jane Price was a student coach with us, she told us about one occasion when she used her new-found deep listening skills on her teenage daughter:

> One of the most rewarding experiences I have had with my coaching was lowering the stroppiness barrier of my teenage daughter. All previous attempts at discussing career choices had resulted in cross, unsatisfactory altercations and cold, gloomy silences as her own frustrations and worries washed over her and I took on the 'Mother knows best' attitude and, of course, my views were more valid than hers! But on this occasion, I reined back my views and asked open questions to explore *her* reality of the situation. I became genuinely interested in what she was saying and *listened* (possibly for the first time!). As I did this, my body relaxed and I noticed that subconsciously I was mirroring her body actions and reflecting back to her using her language. She was truly amazed at the transformation in me and responded with openness. Maintaining calm helped her to keep her concentration as she projected forward to 'her ideal working day' and the tasks that she would really enjoy doing. From these she worked backwards to identify degree subjects that would set her on the path towards her 'ideal'. She was clearer about her options and more motivated to spend time researching them. A good first step!

So as a student coach or a manager/team leader, how on earth do you learn how to reach the kind of listening level of an experienced coach and how will you know when you've reached it? We think there are four types of listening. Consider where you think you spend most of your time.

Superficial listening

This is when you are concentrating on another activity while someone is trying to talk to you. You know they are talking to you, but you are very focused on what is going through your own mind – what you are watching on television or listening to on the radio. This is the kind of listening that happens when your friend is sounding off yet again about her frustrations at work and you've heard it all before but don't want to be rude, so you pretend to listen. You say 'ah ha' and 'yep', hopefully in the right places, but in actual fact you probably couldn't repeat what she has just said to you. Cosmetic listening can be fine if someone just needs to let off steam but it isn't useful in a coaching context when you need to hear all the information a coachee gives you.

Social listening

This is when you are chatting with friends or family. You are all talking over each other, laughing, thinking of a million and one things to say, thinking about things you mustn't forget to do or tell the other person. This is when your own thoughts are most important to you – you are enjoying the interaction with your friends, there is lots going on, noise around you and you are probably doing something while you are talking, be it making coffee, eating, watching other people, keeping an eye on small children. It is a balance between talking and listening and internally process-ing what we hear so that we can bring into the conversation our own experiences and thoughts. The person you are listening to is likely to want your opinion and they will feel as though they owe you time to talk about yourself as well.

Intentional listening

This is more focused listening. You are making more of an effort to listen than to talk. You are not giving your own opinions or advice. You are not relating stories about your own experiences. You are looking at the person directly, making eye con-tact, nodding but not interrupting. You want to understand what they are saying and to remember the facts they are telling you. You are in their shoes and can see things from their perspective, even if it is different from your own. You are relating to the person who is talking to you by asking clarifying questions, repeating infor-mation back to them and by challenging some of their assumptions. Usually you will be hearing about events in a logical time sequence in the order in which they happened. Often the subject matter will be more serious than usual. You might be talking about something confidential, a problem or a difficulty; either way, this subject is important to your friend and you are respecting that.

We are guessing that you probably spend most of your time in conversational, a little less time in cosmetic and only really gravitate to active listening when the situation is called for. That is quite normal – it is everyday life after all, and if we all walked around listening to others in active listening mode we probably wouldn't get any work done or go anywhere!

We did say there were four main listening levels though and the fourth is where we think coaches should sit for the time they are with their coachees – this is deep listening.

Immersed listening

This is what you need to aim for as a coach and it is to this level of listening that we have devoted this chapter. If you can master this it will make the difference between being a *good* coach and an *outstanding* coach for your female coachees. This is the place where listening is taken to the next level, where you don't just hear what the coachee is saying but instead get a real sense of who they are. At this level of listening you will have little awareness of yourself – your mind is calm and almost meditative with insights about your coachee surfacing as you listen and they talk.

You won't be listening at this level non-stop throughout the entire coaching conversation. You will need to ask for information and ask questions which help your coachee to move forward, but going in and out of deep listening will let you pick up on what is behind your coachee's story. You will listen to what is *not* being said, what is consciously or unconsciously being avoided.

How do you train yourself to listen as a coach? Practice is the key and we have five ways we teach our students to practise their listening skills:

- First of all, in your everyday behaviour, notice which listening level you think you are on and when. Notice when you are meant to be listening more than you are and ask yourself what is getting in the way of listening at a deeper level. Becoming aware of where you listen for most of the time is an eye-opener for our students. In fact, most of us don't listen anywhere near as well as we think we do, but if we've never been challenged to listen we fall out of the habit and the loudest noise we hear for much of the time is our own thoughts. Being a coach doesn't mean you are not allowed those thoughts any more, it simply means that for the time you are with a coachee your own thoughts, worries and concerns need to be put to one side.

- Practise looking at someone and making eye contact when you listen – it will help you to concentrate.

- Practise different strategies to place your thoughts on one side. The more you do it, the easier it will become and you will find a strategy that works for you.

- Practise listening to a family member and talking about something important with them while the television is on in the background. Developing a knack for cutting out background noise will stand you in good stead. It may not always be possible to coach someone in a very quiet room, and both of us have coached people successfully in hotel lounges, cafes and restaurants. If you are confident about your level of listening, you will be able to focus on your coachee and cut out any background noise or distraction.

- When you are next out with someone, practise your listening and ask them for feedback. Tell them what you are doing perhaps and ask them to mark you as to which level they thought you were listening to them on – that will be the real key.

What are your barriers to listening as a coach/manager using a coaching approach?

You are likely to have your own set of barriers to being able to listen effectively. It is not only background noise you have to consider. Think about where you coach. Knowing and handling your environment is an important part of creating the right space to coach. If you're coaching at work, do your colleagues know you can't be disturbed? Is where you're coaching really confidential? Is there any chance that your conversation will be overheard?

In a public place, such as a hotel lounge, cafe or restaurant, choose times to meet your coachee that won't be so busy. Obviously a restaurant in the evening is probably going to be busier than at 11 a.m., so if the staff don't mind you sitting in a corner with your coachee and two coffees, the morning would be a better time. If you choose good quality hotels, mid week, you are more likely to be surrounded by business people having meetings of their own instead of holiday makers or weekenders with noisy children. So think about which hotels near you which might be suitable and which days of the week should be avoided.

These are not the only distractions you might face though. We mentioned above the thoughts that might go through your own mind. If you've had an argument with someone just before the session, for example, you will need to learn how to deal with your feelings so you are able to be professional, to train yourself to focus on your coachee so she has no hint of your personal situation. It is highly unprofessional to bumble in with your story of bureaucracy on the railways, for instance, after a delayed train journey to your appointment. One of our coaches fell over as she was walking across a railway platform to reach a hotel in the middle of London – it was a wet day, her coat was soaked as she had fallen in a puddle and she was a bit shaky. Her coachee would never have known though. She slipped into the ladies, took off her wet coat, draped it over her arm inside out and regained her composure before confidently walking into the lobby, hand outstretched and smiling warmly to greet her coachee. That is all part of being able to listen effectively – to put your own traumas, stories and rants to one side. Remember it is not your session, it is the coachee's.

During a session you might also find interruptions popping into your mind that break your concentration. You might remember you have to call someone immediately after the session or realise you didn't get the chicken out of the freezer, so you will have to buy a fresh one on the way home; whatever it is, you are likely to have a pen and paper with you so jot down one word discreetly so you can take the thought out of your mind and continue your listening. Your coachee won't be aware that you've broken concentration and, with practice, you will be able to pick up your train of thought quickly.

Another barrier to listening might be if your coachee comes with an issue or tells you a story which mirrors something that is going on in your own life – this does seem to happen a lot! How much do you give away that you understand where they are coming from? Will telling your coachee that you are going through something similar help them? No is our answer and furthermore it will break the coaching space and your train of thought. There are very few situations we can think of where it would be appropriate to tell a coachee that you have experienced something similar. A knowing nod or smile can say a thousand words and could give your coachee a little comfort, making it clear that they are not the only one in the world who has been through a particular experience. Remember, their take on the event, their thoughts and the way they will deal with it will be entirely different to your own or that of your other coachees. It is therefore of no help to regale the coachee with how you or someone else dealt with it. Wondering whether to say anything at this juncture will simply break your concentration and listening level; if in doubt, stick to the coaching, ask open questions and keep your genuine interest in your coachee's opinion to the fore.

If you are worrying about what you will say next, it is fatally easy to stop listening and jump in too soon based on what your coachee first tells you. Don't assume you know where the conversation is heading. This can lead to confusion because you haven't heard the whole story so keep listening until you have the full picture.

Our best advice is to concentrate on the coachee, not yourself. Worrying about looking good or showing off your superb coaching skills means you are not listening. Leave your ego outside the coaching space!

Ineke Buskens says:

> Listening to women, really listening to women, means listening to what is said and how it is said, but also listening to what is not said. It will be very important to listen carefully to what is said 'between the lines' and observe non-verbal communication ... and to hold 'a space of not yet understanding' for a while because it is important not to make sense too soon. (2009: 4)

The simple rules are:

- If you are talking, you are not listening.

- If you are preparing what to say next, you are not listening.

- If you are butting in, you are not listening.

- If you are using hand signals to communicate with someone whilst on the phone with someone else, you are not listening.

Just one more obvious interruption ... your mobile. Both you and your coachee should turn off your mobiles before beginning the coaching session. There is nothing worse than just getting to the crux of a situation or a breakthrough moment with a coachee and having their phone (or worse yours) beeping.

Do remember to listen with your eyes as well as your ears. If your coachee is telling you she is perfectly relaxed about having her mother-in-law come to live with her, but she has her jaw clenched and her shoulders up by her ears, you'd need to challenge her. If she says she is motivated and ready to change things at work, but is sitting slumped with her arms folded protectively across her chest, you'd be right to doubt her enthusiasm. If there is a mismatch between what you hear and what you see, it is usually the non-verbal language that is telling the truth.

If you are coaching your coachee over the phone you need to 'double listen'. You should be listening to the words but also paying attention to your coachee's tone of voice – changes in speed or volume all give clues about whether she really means what she says.

And don't forget your own body language, especially over the phone. Look alert, be alert, be focused and interested – your coachee will know if you aren't.

Listening and note taking

When you are first learning to coach it is natural to panic about whether you will remember everything your coachee tells you, but trying to write it all down actually stops you from listening. If your coachee is in full flow, the last thing you want is to keep stopping her so you can catch up with your note taking. If you really listened to a friend for a couple of hours over coffee, you'd be able to remember everything she said to regale someone else with wouldn't you? With just a few words or phrases, you will remember – it is not imperative to take down every word, which would be a massive distraction.

We find that with practice, you will jot down just a few notes, enough to remind you what has been said, without even breaking eye contact with your coachee.

Of course there can be times during a coaching session when it is entirely appropriate to make detailed notes. Suppose your coachee has decided on five things to do before the end of the week; recording those specific details while she lists them will feel very different to taking notes all the time she is speaking.

If writing isn't for you, you could try using a small netbook. You will need to be a touch typist to make the most of this but the screen is small so it won't create a barrier between you and your coachee and can work very effectively.

Some students ask about recording sessions. This is very much down to personal choice but do think about possible technical mishaps or whether recording equipment might inhibit your coachee. Also while you can easily flick through written notes to find a detail you want to check, it might take longer to search for it on a recording.

As well as helping you to remember points during a session, use your notes to refresh your memory of past sessions before you next see your coachee. You are not acting like a teacher, checking that their homework has been done, but if your coachee has said she wants to phone six possible new coachees, start a blog and have leaflets printed before you next meet, it is helpful to remind yourself of the details so you don't start the next session looking blank.

It is also usually a requirement of your professional insurance cover that you keep a record of your sessions with coachees. In fact they may tell you to keep these records on file for up to seven years. Apart from implementing insurance requirements, these records are a lifesaver when a coachee comes back to you for further coaching after a gap of a couple of years or more. If this happens you will probably be surprised how much you do remember about them, but being able to check up on the detail is really helpful.

Listening for a connection

A useful way to build rapport with your coachee and to help her feel heard is to notice a connection between the words she uses to describe things. Most people tend to favour certain groups of words; for instance, some people use words that describe 'feeling' sensations, which are known as *kinaesthetic*. Others favour words that depict *visual* images and others use their sense of hearing (i.e. they are *auditory* when they describe the world). While it is fair to say that we use a mixture of all our senses, most people choose one over the other two for much of the time. If you can decipher which sense your coachee prefers, use similar language back to her, and match her tonality and pace; she will recognise the connection. In essence, what we are saying is that if your coachee uses kinaesthetic language a lot (e.g. 'it feels fine to me', 'she's a pain in the neck', 'it gives me a warm glow') and you reply with auditory phrases (e.g. 'that sounds good to me', 'I've heard it all before'), you may not quite gel together and the conversation won't feel completely natural. What you want for an ideal coaching session is a sense of being on the same wavelength and finding a connection; language is one way to do that.

Listening and drawing

Sometimes when we are deep in conversation with a coachee it is very helpful to use drawings to illustrate what the coachee is talking about. Remember Key Principle 5, that women are very visual, so this method of ensuring coach and coachee are on the right track is perfect for your female coachee. Drawing pictures also helps to clarify the situation your coachee finds herself in. However, don't overcomplicate what we mean by drawing here – we mean stick pictures not Van Gogh!

One coachee, we'll call her Mary, came to a session to understand how she always ended up being taken down a road she didn't want to go down. She described how her friends would talk her into going places she didn't really want to go. They would either assume she had said yes or lead her, through their conversation, into saying yes. Either way, this happened all too often and she wanted to change her behaviour – she just didn't know how. She always gave in to what she called 'emotional blackmail' and once she had agreed to do something Mary always stood by her word, so backing out wasn't an option.

Her coach asked her to pinpoint the exact moment in the conversation where she thought she had made the decision to say yes. Once she thought about it, she realised that she generally agreed to do something several sentences earlier than when she got the conscious feeling of 'I've done it again!' Her coach picked up on the phraseology she had used several times of 'being taken down a road she didn't want to go down'. She drew two lines on a piece of paper that represented a road and showed it to Mary before asking, 'So if this is the road your friends want you to go down, how do you remind yourself not to go down it?' To the coach's surprise, she said, 'I'd have to put a roundabout in!' The coach then drew a roundabout in the middle of the road. This is what she drew:

Seeing the road and the roundabout as an actual picture was a major milestone in the coaching session. The coach then asked how many exits there should be off the roundabout. The coachee said just one. She took the picture from the coach and drew the new road where she wanted it. This is what she drew:

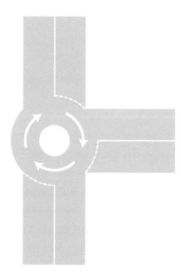

Mary could now see another option (i.e. another road that she could choose to go down). Then the coach asked her, 'OK, so imagine you're having a conversation where you'd usually be taken down a road you don't want to go down. Given that you now have a roundabout and another road that you could choose, how will you stop yourself going down the road you don't want to?' The coachee smiled and said, 'I'd put in some traffic lights just before the roundabout to remind me to stop and come up with an answer I feel comfortable with. If I have traffic lights there and they are on red, they'll remind me to stop and think before I speak.' In fact, during the session Mary went on to identify a phrase she would feel comfortable saying to refuse offers she didn't want, and she used this very well in practice.

On another occasion, a coachee, we'll call her Bridget, was talking about how she sometimes felt that she under-performed. She described having a level at which she would like to perform at and how although sometimes she meets that level, at other times she feels she falls short, which leaves her feeling bad about herself. At this point, the coach drew the following diagram:

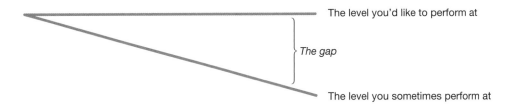

The coach drew this diagram in front of the coachee to clarify that she understood correctly. She asked her if the visual image reflected how she felt – she didn't presume she had got the image right but checked first. Bridget instantly saw a connection between how she was feeling and the image the coach had drawn. She later said: 'Seeing a physical representation of what I'd described meant that it made much more sense and that finding the way to plug the gap became more obvious. I have a real affinity for illustrations such as these and I've used them with my staff before now to great effect. I think they're a hugely important self development tool and having that meant that I could look at it after the session, and take in what it meant to me.' The next part of the coaching session focused on asking Bridget how she might choose to plug that gap. The coachee came up with three things she would do differently to make sure that her level of performance remained as straight and as on target as possible.

Being able to doodle, if you like, to illustrate what your coachees are saying will make a big difference. Remember that your interpretation may not be exactly as your coachee sees it. If you draw something always check with them: 'This is how it seems to me – have I got that right?' If it isn't, correct the drawing until it is exactly how the coachee sees it and how it makes sense to them.

Listening 'in the moment' and keeping up with the conversation regardless of what is happening around you is all part of your job and your profession. You listen for someone's values and dreams, for what inspires them, for who they really are. It is simply something for which you will need to develop a genuine skill.

6 Negotiating Negativity

In our experience, when a woman feels negative it can affect her on many levels. Self doubt, questioning her decisions, feeling as though others are 'getting at her' can cause emotions to run high and a woman's sense of self can be put on the line. The thing with negativity though is that mostly it seems to be in the eye (or mind) of the holder. You will speak to one woman in an incredibly stressful or negative situation and while she might be sad or disappointed, she will be utterly determined that change can happen; positive that whatever happens she will be OK and even confident that she will come out the other side with class, grace and strength. For another, the same situation could see them tumbling into a vortex of put-downs and spinning out of control with little or no expectation of being able to recover. It isn't healthy, but it does happen to most women at some point in their lives, even the strong, successful ones. Calm and collected they may seem on the outside but inside they will be fighting a hard internal battle. Both these women could become your coachees.

You'd think it would be easy to tell Ms Positive from Ms Negative, wouldn't you? Women can be very good at putting on the make-up, the dress, the high heels and the smile to hide how crushingly devastated they feel. Do you remember the scene in the film *Love Actually* where Emma Thompson's character Karen realises that her husband is having an affair? The recognition dawns on her while she is unwrapping Christmas presents under the tree with her husband and children. She cheerfully excuses herself before climbing the stairs, shutting herself in the bedroom and falling apart. What happens next is a powerful illustration of what it sometimes takes to be a woman. In this fictional example, and in real life, it is a woman's natural instinct to protect the feelings of others around her that means she can do this. A woman will absorb pain, grief, regret, disappointment and anger and keep it hidden from view to maintain balance, peace and safety for others. Women around the world watched Karen straighten herself up, wipe her tears, take deep breaths and steady herself to run downstairs full of energy, smiles and Christmas excitement as she whisks her family off to a Christmas school play. We are willing to bet that every woman who saw that scene identified with it and knew that strength. Women do put on a brave face; it is part of the 'disproportionate degree of self sacrifice that women are willing to make on behalf of those they love' (Gilbert 2010: 171).

At home, alone, we can see how some women might deal with their own negativity, but what happens in the more public setting of the workplace? We asked Sarah Owens, Managing Director of an all-female team at London recruitment agency Direct Recruitment, what effect she thinks negativity has on women. She says: 'I think it's actually much harder for a woman who is feeling negative to hide her feelings in an all-woman office because women are naturally more attuned to moods.'

A study of women-led businesses found that 'women brought an "intuitive" insight to bear on the emotional problems of the staff – an intuition which is simply a woman's superior interest in her fellow human beings' (Moir and Jessel, 1998: 173).

Most importantly, we read that vital sign – body language: 'Women, because of the way their brains are wired, bring an extra element of emotional sensitivity into the equation' (Moir and Jessel, 1998: 170).

Sarah Owens adds: 'If someone's feeling negative, the body language shows it all and the mood can be almost palpable. The other clue will be in *how* things are said, or not said. I think there's a natural tendency for another woman to try to find out what the matter is rather than ignore things, and if someone's annoyed, they will often give the polite one word answer and the tone of voice, plus the limited eye contact – body language again – gives it away. What you do next, of course, is the big question, before things escalate and the negativity spreads, a danger if the issue is something work or work colleague related.'

Sarah brought up several topics that are important to digest. Women 'get' very quickly if something isn't right with someone they know well and they naturally want to put it right. There is that caring and supportive side of a woman's personality again – she genuinely wants everyone around her to feel and to be OK.

Moir and Jessel observe: 'Women, who as girls, chose their friends with much greater, and more committed care (than boys do) try to like the people they work with, understanding their needs, breaking down the barriers of status' (1998: 171).

This is also the opinion of Cambridge University psychologist Simon Baron-Cohen, who comments that: 'the female brain is predominantly hard-wired for empathy' (quoted in Narain, 2010).

As you are training to become a coach, understanding how women instinctively deal with negative situations will be of immense power to you. Our female coachees often come to talk about other people in their lives. If others aren't happy, your coachee will take that on board to try to help. As we discussed above, the natural response of a non-coach will be to give praise and to cajole – reminding her how good she is at the things she does. A non-coach will remind her how situations always get better and that everything will be OK, but that only lasts for a short time. A coach's way of dealing with a coachee who feels negative will be quite different. In the first place, we don't know our coachees as well as their friends – we don't share their history and so we can't tell them how well they've done in the past. What we do is much more powerful though: we get them to tell us and use our skills of reflecting back to help the coachee hear what we are hearing. Here's one way the reflecting back technique could work:

COACHEE: It's not a good time for me at the moment. I'm not productive right now.

COACH: You're not productive?

COACHEE: Well ... I am productive. I mean, I'm really surprised at how much I still do under the circumstance really.

Imagine if this was a friend-to-friend chat – it might have gone like this:

FRIEND 1: It's not a good time for me at the moment. I'm not productive right now.

FRIEND 2: Listen, you're the most productive person I know. If I had half your energy, I'd do ten times more than *I* manage to do.

FRIEND 1: Mmm ... well thanks for the vote of confidence, but I can assure you, it's all fake!

Can you see the difference? In the friends' scenario, Friend 1 doesn't take Friend 2 seriously and Friend 2 has discredited Friend 1's opinion of herself, even though it is well intentioned. With the coaching example, however, her coach took her feeling of unproductivity seriously and, as a result, with just one clarification, the coachee saw the areas where she had managed to be productive.

One thing we would like to point out at this juncture is that negativity in a coachee isn't always a bad thing. We spoke to Gordon Melvin, one of our coaches and an expert in the Enneagram, an ancient personality typology model. He explains that we need to feel negative sometimes in order to assess our situation and make the right decisions for us:

> Behind every human activity, decision, and process, there are three forces (part of what is often referred to as universal law). We can easily recognise these constant companions with the all too familiar name of the first two forces – 'yes' and 'no'. The 'positive' and 'negative' forces are involved with everything we do and every corner we turn. Both are essential to life and without the negative we could never be positive, they are mutual forces in relation to each other and essential to each other. The 'negative' or the 'no' stands to challenge us as we pause to consider what we are doing – without the 'no' or the 'negative' we would actually be inert. The extent of our positive energy or our negative energy is in exact relation to the other – they go hand in hand. For the most part when we come to the 'yes' or 'no' in our decision, work, or process, we takes sides at the expense of one of these forces, thinking we have put the negative or positive away, but they will reveal their necessary heads at every interval along the way!

> On another level there is another force … that is for the most part, unobserved in our process, which brings the extreme of the 'yes' and the 'no' into a new and exciting balance. This is where something inside the psyche observes the apparent conflict of interests between the tug of war of the 'yes' and 'no' and through careful attentive observation, reconciles the two in a new and harmonious way. This is the third force. These three forces are often referred to as affirming (yes), denying (no) and reconciling (the third force in the equation). When we take both the 'yes' and the 'no' into the equation we get a whole new slant on things and a new creative and dynamic energy is released.

The reason we mention this is that it is important not to be hell-bent on helping your coachee see the positive, but instead to support her decision making process with the positive, the negative and the weighing up of the two, the reconciliation.

There is no doubt that if someone feels negative over a prolonged period of time that negativity has a habit of creeping into their thoughts and unconscious, which could cause problems in previously harmonious areas of life. Perhaps one thing goes wrong and it dents our positivity or confidence, then maybe something else happens and then something else – in a short space of time, if negativity isn't dealt with or noticed, it can seep into every area of our lives leaving us feeling pretty despondent. When a coachee comes to see you, they probably know they feel negative, but they may not always realise the extent to which that pessimism is affecting other areas of their lives.

How should a coach deal with negativity? Well, remember good quality, ethical coaching is not prescriptive – it is not about stroking your chin in a thought provoking manner as you summarise that your coachee's problem is their negativity. It is about everything you've read so far. It is about being specific, understanding what your coachee wants from the session, how your coachee feels or perceives her situation and how she'd like to perceive it. It is about honing in on what specifically would make the difference to her by the end of the session. Part of your skill set is listening to her, properly and completely. Your job is asking questions that cut swiftly to the chase and giving your coachee the chance to answer. Your job is to ask the simplest and most probing questions. Your job is to reflect back what you hear and what you see.

Our example shows how to deal with what you hear, but what about what you see? When a coachee walks into your coaching room how do you know what mood she is in? How can you tell whether she is confident, full of energy and excited about the prospects her coaching session might bring or whether she has lost her way, is nervous about exposing her vulnerability to a coach and unsure of what the session will uncover? We will talk more about body language later, but it is important to link body language and tone of voice directly to negativity because they are your tell-tale signs – and missing those signs will do your female coachee a huge injustice.

The way she moves, sits and walks into the room gives you immediate signals as to her mood. Slouching, folded arms across the chest, hunching over a little (trying to make herself appear smaller) are all signs that this woman doesn't want to be seen, that she isn't open to positivity, that she feels bad about something. In stark contrast, you will know if she is happy and confident as she will breeze into the room and stand up straight – her presence can be felt. She will have an air of positivity and confidence around her. Then there is the woman who is hiding how bad things are. Her body language will to a great extent show someone confident, standing tall and having a presence – but the giveaway will be her eyes. Her eyes will tell you instantly if her body language is genuine or not, and her tone of voice will give away her mood.

A woman who diminishes the volume of her voice or who refuses to say very much may be feeling negative, but a stronger more authoritative voice can just as easily be negative. If you sense sarcasm, if you keep your ear out for 'yes but's' or for repetition of negative language, you will know.

During a face-to-face session, notice how her body language changes when you talk about certain issues – for instance, talking about family might mean that she relaxes, that her language is excited and feels positive. Switch the topic to her boss, for example, and all that could change. Notice those changes and reflect them back to your coachee. Over the telephone, you will listen to tone far more, as well as silence, the speed of her voice and the breaths she takes. Practice will give you the same information from listening to her voice as a face-to-face session would when you had both body language and visual cues to take into the equation.

One coachee we saw actually shuddered visibly when she spoke about a particular incident at work. When her coach pointed it out to her, she had no idea at all that she had just shuddered! The fact that she became aware of it made her more determined to deal with the situation swiftly. We often fail to see our own body language or hear our tone of voice, especially when we are feeling low and lacking in energy.

Identifying negative thoughts, feelings or expectations is the very first step to being able to help your coachee move forward and bring some elements of positivity back into her life. Sitting with your coachee with their negativity for a short while certainly gives your coachee validity and lets them know that you are seeing their story from their point of view. When we say 'sitting with their negativity', we mean that it is perfectly OK to recognise how negative a situation is. If you are a truly interested, focused and empathetic coach this will be easy to do. This is not about faking interest but making genuine comments such as:

❚ **'I can see that's been really difficult'**

or

❚ **'That really seems to have affected lots of areas of your life'**

that will show that you recognise their negativity and, at the same time, will point out to them the level of negativity they appear to be experiencing. Remember, coaching is not simply a stream of questions; it is interaction with another human being, noticing how difficult a situation seems to have been for your coachee and, empathising, without getting emotionally involved or being unprofessional, that is going to enhance your relationship with your coachee. Don't forget Key Principle 1, that women want to feel their relationship with their coach is unique and different from the coach's relationship with other coachees.

So, you've noticed that your coachee is feeling negative, and you may also have observed what lines of conversation specifically make your coachee's body language or tone of voice change, but what do you do with it now?

There are a few exercises you could take your coachee through. However, in the spirit of not being directive, persuasive or prescriptive, always offer exercises without expectation. They may say no, which would be perfectly acceptable and then you would continue with the coaching session and the TGROW model. If they say yes, you could show them a range of tools they might like to try. For instance, you would never say:

❚ **'Right then, we're going to do this today ...'**

Instead you'd say:

> **'OK, well if I outline a couple of the exercises that you could use, would you like to let me know which ones, if any, sound interesting to you?'**

What this says is, 'You don't have to do any of these, but if you are looking for an external tool to help you out of this phase in your life, we can work with that.' You are constantly reinforcing that the direction of the session is the coachee's and not yours.

We use three tools that work very well and that we teach our students. As you read through and start to understand them, have a think about the ones that might work for you.

1 Understanding how the unconscious mind works and reprogramming negative thoughts with positive thoughts

The unconscious mind is a very complex part of us. There is much that is unknown about how it works and functions and there are many books on the subject that will be extremely helpful if this is an area you'd like to know more about. In terms of using the unconscious mind with your coaching coachees, it will be enough to recognise that it seems to act rather like the hard drive on your computer, storing information we've absorbed in our past. We've all smelt a familiar aroma which has taken us back to a memory from long ago, we've all heard words or phrases and been reminded of someone who said them, we've all seen images or objects that we know we've seen before but seemed to have forgotten. All of that information informs how we react to situations today. If 80% of those images, words and smells link to positive events, we might be quite a naturally optimistic person. This is because when we come across a word, phrase, situation, smell or someone who reminds us of another individual, 80% of what is locked in our unconscious mind is positive, so the thoughts we've attached to those things will be predominantly positive. However, if the large majority of your hard drive is negative then you are more likely to react pessimistically to phrases, images and situations than your friend with 80% positive programming. Ultimately the unconscious mind is all about programming. It might be helpful to ask if this is something your coachee might be interested in knowing about. You might find it beneficial to let them know how the unconscious mind seems to work with negative and positive thoughts, but be aware that this is something that won't fit every coachee.

By offering it as a tool, you are giving the coachee the option of refusing, which is perfect for a non-directional coaching session. Ask a question such as:

> **'Would it be helpful to understand how negativity can affect our decisions?'**

or

> **'The unconscious mind can be used as a helpful tool – would you like to know more about that?'**

Notice how these questions are closed questions. You are after permission here – you want to know one way or the other – so closed questions are perfect.

If your coachee says yes, they would like to see how this tool works, you can demonstrate it very simply by drawing a circle on a sheet on paper and dividing the circle into two halves – with one side labelled as the unconscious mind and the other side as the conscious mind.

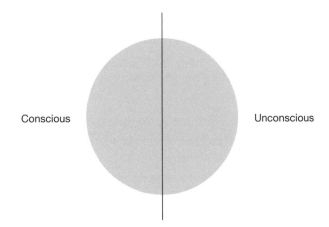

Conscious   Unconscious

You can then explain that the unconscious seems to act as our hard drive, collecting all of the thoughts we think, the images we see, the words we hear and the feelings we feel. It is where the conscious mind appears to go to retrieve information. If that is indeed the case then the more negativity in that bank, the more chance we have of retrieving negativity. If it is filled with positive thoughts, it is easier to find something positive.

If your coachee is interested in this and wants to understand how to reprogramme a negative unconscious to being predominantly positive, there is an exercise they could try.

You should point out at this stage that if your coachee decides to try this, they need to persevere for at least two weeks before it might become more comfortable. It needs a little focus, but in our experience it is entirely possible.

The five step process we have identified is as follows:

i   Your coachee will need to start recognising when their language is negative and when it is positive. How they do that is entirely up to them. Some of our coachees have even gone as far as jotting down a pen mark in their diary when they think negatively and then adding them up at the end of the day. For others, it will be completely different so ask your coachee how they would choose to start recognising their own negative language and work with that.

ii   Each time your coachee has recognised a negative phrase or thought pattern they will need to identify its exact positive opposite. For instance, if they think 'Red lights make me so late', they would need to find a phrase to turn that into a positive. It could be 'Red lights alow me precious time to think' – your coachee should choose their own.

iii   This is where your coachee is most likely to flag up their doubts about this process because they will tell you that they don't believe their new positive phrase. And it is true, they don't. But this stage of the exercise is not about believing it – it is about replacing negative terms in their mindset with positive ones instead. Believing it isn't necessary. It is simply a replacement opportunity and an exercise in reprogramming.

iv   Now they are going to need a trigger to remember to do this. It is all very well coming up with a wonderful plan about replacing negative with positive thoughts in the safety of a coaching session – your coachee might even be excited about it – but once they get back to children, bosses, partners, shopping and dinner to cook, their nice new positive thinking plan could go right out of the window. They will need a trigger. What would theirs be? It will be completely different to what yours might be, so ask them directly:

> **'How are you going to remember to do this?'**
>
> **'What is going to be your trigger for your new thought process?'**
>
> **'When are you most likely to remember to do this?'**

Notice how they are all open questions. You want to elicit information – you want their opinions and thoughts on how they will make this work. You need their emotional buy-in. Each coachee will come up with their own take and it is always interesting to hear about another person's trigger – our coachees have come up with all kinds of wonderful ways to remember, from putting Post-it notes all around their home or office to pictures of beaches on car dashboards. What would your coachee do?

v   Lastly, what is her motivation? Once again, in the comfort of a coaching session her motivation can be clear and strong. When she leaves your office, it can easily slip away. At this point it is helpful to ask your coachee how they are motivated. Most of us either respond to moving towards something positive (the carrot – a reward based method: 'If I do this, something good will happen') or by moving away from something negative (the stick – a worst case scenario: 'If I don't do this, something negative will happen').

One of our students, James Carter, came up with a brand new motivation when we taught this – he said he was a 'carrick' (i.e. in some situations motivated by positivity and in some situations motivated by negativity). Your coachee could also be a carrick! It just goes to show, never presume anything. Ask instead and then delve to find out why they would go to the bother of reprogramming their minds. It is going to require some effort and thought so they are going to need a pretty good reason to do this and stick to it – you can help them to cement this as part of your session.

Another of our students, Sophie Eld, went through this exercise in a coaching session and she wrote a post for the UK Coaching Partnership blog (www. ukcoachingpartnership.typepad.com) on her experience:

Magic on M25

Two hours before I reached the M25 I was ensconced in a coaching session with Lynette Allen. We were looking at positive and negative thoughts and coming to the conclusion I needed to 'bank' more positive thoughts. 'You don't have to believe them', Lynette pointed out. Well that's a relief.

This concept of negative thoughts translating into negative beliefs which in turn negatively affect your life is not a new one to me. As I explained to Lynette, I would spot a negative thought but rather than turn it into something positive I would get distracted. 'Oh no, that's a negative thought', I'd think, 'how negative of me'. 'Oh no, that's negative too, now I've doubled my negativity, I'm such a failure'. You can guess what comes next. 'A failure? That's even more negative ...' cue the trip switch. Stop thinking about this. La la la la. Kittens, imagine cute fluffy kittens or something. Anything will do, just move on.

Half an hour before I reached the M25 I saw the first sign. M25 JUNCTIONS 23–19 LONG DELAYS. Oh dear. I had 150 miles to cover to get home and this wasn't a good sign. Figuratively or literally. I continued on, hoping it might relate to travellers heading south rather than me. The rain kept falling and the tyres kept rolling and then there was another sign. M25 JUNCTIONS 23–16 LONG DELAYS. Evidently it was getting worse. Maybe I would be getting off before junction 23. I rather wished I paid more attention to junction numbers rather than always going by name.

Another few miles and I was joining the M25 right in the middle of the obligatory roadworks. The first overhead board warned me again. ACCIDENT. JUNCTION 23–16 40 MIN DELAYS. There goes my theory that 'long delays' might not be as bad as they were making out. The next junction was number 27 and, according to the satnav, I had 44 miles to go. My hopes that I might make a miraculous escape were dashed. Proceeding through the 50 mph roadworks, I resigned myself to the delay. At least it was good processing time for the coaching session, right?

ACCIDENT. JUNCTION 25–16. 40 MIN DELAYS. I'd be joining the back of it even sooner then. My thoughts were glum. Negative even. I spotted them, recognising that this was supposed to be my trigger for manually banking positive thoughts. Positive thoughts that supposedly attract a positive experience of life based on the meta-physical law of attraction. I'd read about it plenty of times. Okay, I thought defiantly, here's my positive thought – there will be no queue ahead. I'll have smooth, plain driving all the way home. Yeah, right, I scoffed. 'You don't have to believe the thoughts', I heard Lynette's voice in my mind. That was when I decided to give it a chance.

Junction 26. I drove past a long queue of people making their escape. I was the rat sitting at the stern, watching all his shipmates diving into the water. Smooth journey I told myself. Steady pace. No stopping.

Junction 25. I was expecting a sea of brake lights at any second but I kept up my mantra. Steady pace. Flowing traffic. 'You don't have to believe it'. Good.

Junction 23. The overhead signs now reported JUNCTION 19–15. LONG DELAYS. They were adamant. I wasn't. How could I possibly expect open roads despite all the expert evidence to the contrary? 'You don't have to believe it'.

Junction 21. So far, so good. I'm visualising the flowing roads ahead. I'm grateful for each mile of movement but still expecting to come upon queues at any moment.

Junction 20. What if the missing queues are because all those people got off and have nothing to do with my positive thinking? So? Does it matter when the end result is exactly what I'm asking for? I guess not.

Junction 19. No queues yet and they were supposed to have started. Could I be lucky enough to escape? Surely not. Maybe it isn't going to be as bad as it could have been though. That'd be great. I return to my positive mantras.

Junction 18. Traffic still flowing. I'm thinking that if this comes off, I'll have to tell Lynette.

Junction 17. No queues in sight despite the continued warnings from the overhead boards. It's really happening. I keep up the positives, trying to drown out the part of me that thinks I'm tempting fate by noticing that everything's going well.

Junction 16. I'm turning off the M25 and I haven't stopped once. This is an experience I have to share. I grin as the title for this blog post pops into my mind.

M40. Hmm. What's next?

2 Negative/positive circle

This is perfect for highlighting how negative thoughts can impact on our actions. Each and every one of us has our own methodical ways of behaving in certain situations, but it is not always easy for us to see how we behave. Rather like the reflecting back tool you've been using up until now, this is a visual reflection of that – and is perfect for your female coachees given Key Principle 5, that women are able to use visualisation very effectively.

Here's the template, which you will find on the accompanying CD:

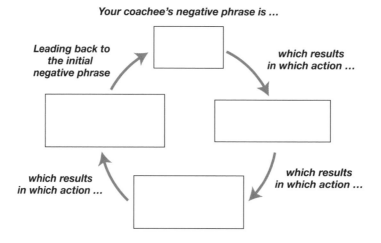

Work through this diagram with your coachee. Ask them to identify one of their favourite negative phrases. Then ask what action comes as a result of thinking that, then what action comes next, then what action comes next. The last action point is certain to result in the coachee having proof for their initial negative phrase and thinking it again – linking the action points and phrases up in one circle.

Here's a completed example:

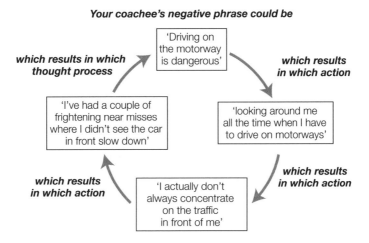

Now let's turn that example on its head to be positive. Ask your coachee what the opposite of their negative phrase would be and work from there.

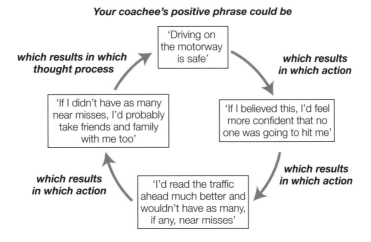

So you see how this works: if your coachee usually follows a negative path, the positive side is all theory; it is all about how she *thinks* she might react if she thought more positively. It gives her an idea, a taster if you like, about how her actions might be different if her thoughts changed. At this stage it is all up to your coachee whether she is prepared to take this model back into her life and try working with it in everyday situations. Do remember to always start with a negative circle and finish on a positive one.

3 Changing state

Changing state is about physically moving. It is about the very act of finding yourself displaying negative body language because of the topic you are talking about and making the decision to change that state of mind. If you decide to change your body language to something more positive, your state of mind will also follow and change. If the tone of your coaching session is particularly negative, you could ask if your coachee would like to stand up, shake out their limbs, get a glass of water or if they would like to change their sitting position for the rest of the session. If they are on the phone, you can still do this – for example, by asking them which room they are in and whether they would like to move to a different room for the solutions part of the session. Changing state is about using the physical space around you to help shift mood and state of mind.

Once you see your coachee's negative state disappearing, bring it to their attention. Sentences that start 'I've noticed that ...' or 'Have you noticed how your body language has changed? You're sitting up straighter ...' will reflect back what you are seeing.

So there you have it – three excellent tools to move your coachees from negativity to positivity. The chances are that one of these will hit a note with your coachee and she will feel drawn to finding out about more of them.

If your coachee doesn't feel that the exercises are for her, a phrase such as:

> **'OK, so now I've heard a bit about what is going on for you at the moment, how would you like to use today's session?'**

will be productive. This is when you encourage your coachee to redefine or clarify her goals for the session. You can influence her body language to change and her tone of voice to alter by doing it yourself – by sitting up straighter, smiling or taking a deep breath, your tone will be brighter and possibly more convictional and positive about the future.

What if a coachee is struggling with becoming more positive?

It is very difficult to coach someone who doesn't want to feel more positive, but it may be that they just find it hard to recognise the potential for a better outcome. By asking the following question you are not forcing them to believe that things *will* get better (after all, that is your opinion and not theirs), but you are asking if they are prepared to look at the *prospect* of the situation improving. You could ask:

▌ **'Out of 10, how positive do you feel that you can turn this around?'**

A great follow-up question if that figure is low (say a 2 out of 10) is:

▌ **'How important is it to you that we move that score up today?'**

Yes, you are presuming that the score should be moving in the upwards direction, but your coachee has come for a coaching session and that is what coaching is about. What you are *not* doing here is presuming that the coachee has to reach a 10 by the end of the session to feel it has been helpful. Your coachee may think that is unrealistic and a 3 may be where they see themselves heading – that is fine, it is their session and their life – moving one point up for some people is all they can take on. Over time this tends to change, but slow progress is still progress.

7 Body Language and Image in a Woman's World

We all know what body language is but does it really matter that much? It is widely documented that communication is made up of three elements: body language, tone of voice and speech. The words that come out of our mouths may not always tell the truth, but our bodies speak for us all the time, whether we want them to or not. Unless we make a conscious effort to control our body language, we are continually telling people how we feel and think by our physical movements. Our posture, gestures, movements and facial expressions as well as our tone of voice, vocal inflections and the speed at which we speak, often 'talk' more accurately and truthfully than the words coming out of our mouths. Every movement reveals if we are impatient, uneasy, angry, happy or excited, whatever we may say in words. If you've had a bad day, your hunched shoulders and subdued tone of voice will say that you are tense, no matter how much you insist 'I'm fine'.

So, if body language says so much, what can you tell from a woman's body language in particular? In our experience of teaching and coaching we find that there are two distinct ways in which a woman's body language is very different to a man's. Firstly, have you noticed any differences in the way in which men and women take up space? Typically men sit well back in a chair, legs apart and using all the available space. A woman is much more likely to squeeze herself into a smaller area. Traditionally women were told to take up as little space as possible both physically and in 'air time' – in other words, how frequently they put forward their own opinions.

Jane Fonda once observed how owning the space you are in can be a particular challenge for women: 'I continue to be amazed at the number of women who I consider strong leaders who still worry about taking up too much space in meetings' (quoted in Goyder, 2009: 147).

As you go through your day, you may start to notice that some of your female friends and colleagues aren't 'owning' the space around them and their body language will give that away. Clues such as a woman looking towards the floor, having her arms crossed in front of her body or fiddling with her hair, could all be signs that she's not owning her space – possibly because she feels uncomfortable. Maybe she has a hand covering her mouth or is talking very quietly. If you notice these signs during a session you could help instantly by putting the coachee at ease. Explain what will be happening in the session, what time it will start and finish, ask her if she would like a cup of tea, coffee or water (if you are meeting her face to face) or if your session is telephone based, check with her that she is comfortable and won't be disturbed for the hour. Imagine you are inviting her into your own home, even if you're coaching a colleague: being warm, welcoming and confident will help her take your lead. The most important way of putting your coachee at ease is by reassuring her that this is her space to use as she wishes and everything she says is confidential; this is of paramount importance of course if you're coaching within the workplace.

As the session progresses and she tells you about the reality of her situation, it may be helpful to ask what body language she uses in certain situations. If she says she doesn't feel listened to in meetings, for instance, or that her family don't take any notice of her, this is the perfect opportunity to ask, 'Tell me how you think you're standing or sitting on those occasions?' Body language is likely to come into play more than your coachee thinks, so it is an interesting area.

The second gender difference we've noticed is in how conscious women are of their image. That is not to say that men don't care about theirs, but it does seem that women feel judged on the physical impression they make far more than their male counterparts. Your female coachee may be a little more self conscious, not sure what to do with her hands or how to sit while she is talking to you, so reassure with your own body language and put her at ease. Make sure you don't fidget, that you are displaying a confident but not intimidating posture, and a calm yet focused demeanour. Certainly, being very aware of both your body language and your female coachee's body language is a vital part of your coaching toolkit.

What would you think if a woman walked into the room with her shoulders hunched, her eyes lowered and barely making eye contact with you and taking small steps as you show her to her chair – what would her body language be saying to you? Now imagine another woman walking into the room – she is smiling, she holds her hand out to shake yours, she warmly meets your eye as she strides to her chair, she looks around her, taking in the contents of the room before making herself comfortable. What is her body language saying to you?

So does body language say everything we need to know? Our first woman comes across as unsure of herself, unclear possibly even as to why she is having coaching, a little shy, not very confident and perhaps we might make a judgement that she is negative about some aspect of her life situation. Meanwhile we assume our second woman to be happy with herself, pleased to be here, confident in her approach to her life, open and receptive to being coached and probably with a list of things she would tell you about herself straight off. But would we be right?

UK Coaching Partnership trained Carole Dodd coaches women, and one of her coachees was our second woman. Carole's first impression of her was 'a lady with confidence', who could move what she wanted in her own life and carry out her plans with ease, but it wasn't long into the coaching process before she realised her initial perceptions might have been wrong. 'Some women', says Carole, 'wear a uniform for who they want others to see.' In this case, our second woman's uniform was a smart image, wearing clothes which suited her body shape, in colours that coordinated, delicate but definitive make-up and a smile to match. 'It turns out', explains Carole, 'that her smart, confident persona was her uniform and in actual fact, the person she felt she was inside didn't match the body language or the image she displayed.' It seems she had become an expert in using what is usually unconscious behaviour and had made a deliberate effort to manipulate her body language to hide an image of herself that she didn't want others to see. What was uncovered during the coaching process was a woman who wasn't sure who she was, who had lost her identity and her way in her own life. Carole reported that her body language actually got progressively worse over the subsequent coaching sessions and that it wasn't until her coachee started to understand who she was inside that her body language began to recover. As Carole's coachee started to appreciate who she was on the inside, and how to project that person on the outside, the two images began to match. Her coachee reported feeling 'genuine' at this point and 'truly confident' in her approach to life. She no longer felt as though she had to mask who she was on the inside with a particular 'uniform', instead, she *is* that uniform. Now that feels quite different.

So what does this teach us about women and their body language?

- Women have the ability to 'mask' how they feel with their body language to some degree, which means that face value isn't always the best judge.

- Image and body language are interlinked with women to a much greater extent than with men.

There are two further important points to make at this juncture: (1) your job is *not* to presume you know what is going on in your coachee's mind even if her body language suggests that she is either brimming with confidence or has none at all, and (2) to understand that women are very good at projecting an image of the person they want others to see – with their body language and with their persona. Women's magazines are full of advice about how to transform ourselves in the belief that 'you have a choice. Who you were yesterday, who you were an hour ago, doesn't have to be the same person as you are now' (Naomie Harris quoted in Goyder, 2009: 87).

In fact, we often play the role that friends or people at work expect of us, so we've become very adept at faking it.

While it is human nature to make snap judgements, this is a part of human nature that coaches are trained to curtail. Why, after all, when we know that a woman is so good at camouflaging her real self, for protection purposes, would we assume that she *is* who her image suggests? Similarly, we also mustn't presume that because a coachee displays the kind of body language that our first woman presented, that she will be negative or despondent to the core. This is about being able to see each coachee for who they are and get to know who they are, without making those judgements that will colour your view of the coaching session. We must also point out that women aren't always hiding their real selves under make-up and sunglasses. During your coaching career you will come across genuinely capable, confident and strong women who chose to use coaching as their back-up to a busy lifestyle, their planning time for multitasking careers and families, and their peace and quiet when their lives are constantly on the go. The key is not to assume anything. Learn to unlearn that habit of presuming, judging and thinking you understand when you only have a small part of her story in front of you.

So now we've ascertained the importance of taking each woman for who she is, how do you get to the core of what your female coachee is really made up of when you've never met her before? How does a coach do this when they have no clue as to her history, her state of mind, her job, her level of happiness with herself or the elements of her life? Well, it starts with building a strong rapport, and this is done first through body language; then you will blend that empathy with the questioning and listening skills you've read about above. Being able to build a rapport with your coachee is essential in the first part of a session and lays the foundations for building a relationship based on truth, honesty and trust. Remember Key Principle 1, that women want to feel their relationship with their coach is unique and different from the coach's relationship with other coachees. This is your chance to make that happen. If you have standard questions and standard methodology, she will know you are the same with all of your coachees. You will lose her before you've even begun. Everything about how you interact with your coachee must be unique and genuinely in-the-moment, then she will know that you are real, that your relationship with her is real and she is not on a production line of coachees.

This is done by building a specific and unique relationship with the coachee the minute she walks into the room or when you pick up the phone. There are four key elements to building an excellent rapport with your female coachee: matching/mirroring, matching mood versus matching energy, making eye contact and nodding.

1 Matching/mirroring

Learning how to use your body language when coaching will mean the difference between working extraordinarily well with your coachees and just working with them.

In everyday circumstances we use our body language almost entirely unconsciously. When we like someone we automatically 'match' or 'mirror' their body language. With someone close, such as a spouse or partner, you will often see a connection because of the way they are sitting, walking or behaving; they will be mirroring and matching each other's stance, sitting position, how they hold their teacup, how they walk. You will have seen older couples who have been together for years moving in the same way, even dressing in similar ways. It is comfortable when someone exhibits the same body language as us; it is quietly reassuring and often says far more than words ever could. The trick to building rapport quickly with your new coachee is to achieve a sense of connection through body language almost instantaneously.

When we build relationships in everyday life, they are developed over a period of months and years. The subtle nuances of matching and mirroring will come with time and closeness. In a coaching situation, you don't have that luxury. Instead you have to be physically and emotionally aware enough to create a connection whereby your coachee feels at ease very quickly.

Matching and mirroring is the process by which you let the coachee know you are on the same wavelength as her. We are naturally attracted to people who are like us. Scientists believe this is because, in evolutionary terms, those individuals who are most like us are the ones who will come to our aid and help us to survive if we are in danger. If your coachee senses that you are like her, the coaching session will shift from 'OK' to 'extraordinary' – the coachee will feel as though you 'get her' and it will be a match. On the face of it, this sounds a little calculating; it is anything but. You will find yourself doing this all the time in everyday life – children do it most easily – as it is a very human way of interacting with another person. Have you ever sat down on your heels to speak to a child so you are the same height as them to find that they've assumed exactly the same position? That child is instinctively mirroring and matching your body language. Have you ever come across someone at work who is upset, hunched over and speaking very quietly? You will find yourself mirroring their body language to encourage them to confide in you.

This is what matching and mirroring is and it is very helpful to bring this to the fore-front of your mind when you are coaching a woman. Think what happens when there is a mismatch of mood. Suppose you phone a firm to complain:

You've taken time off work twice to have furniture delivered and it still hasn't arrived. Their telephone system has asked you to keep pressing options and played you hideous music while they kept you waiting for ten minutes to speak to someone. You are really agitated but the salesperson answers in a laid back soothing tone. You are talking with a sense of urgency and immediacy, the salesperson is speaking slowly and as though they have all day. The more your voice becomes insistent, the more their voice becomes calm. We very much doubt that you would feel taken seriously. They haven't met your energy, they haven't taken you seriously, they don't 'get' what this means to you.

Now imagine this scenario:

The same thing has happened, but when the operator answers, his voice has a sense of purpose to it. You explain the situation, your voice is fast paced, it is clear you want something done now. In return, the salesperson picks up the speed of his voice, matches your energy. You know he is listening to you, you can feel it. How would you feel then? Our guess is that you would feel taken seriously. This is verbal matching and mirroring. It works just as well as visual matching and mirroring.

Mirroring and matching is going to be your number one tool in gaining access to your coachee's real thoughts and, better still, their solutions moving forwards. In short, it is the best technique you have to bring your coachee into the coaching space where the real work can begin.

You have to learn to take more notice of your coachee's body language than you would under normal circumstances and you 'copy' it, for want of a better word. This has to be subtle and the more you practise, the more natural it will become. Copying every move won't go down well, we are sure you can see that, but noticing and mirroring, when done with skill and practice, will work.

The best way to illustrate how this works is to try to picture the exact opposite – what about if your body language was completely different to your coachee's:

Your coachee	*You*
Sitting	Standing
Leaning forward hunched into their knees	Leaning back in your chair
Legs tucked under chair	Legs stretched out in front of you
Arms folded over chest	Hands clasped behind your head
Head down, eyes avoiding contact	Head up, seeking eye contact
Very quiet speech	Loud hearty speech

Can you see how difficult it would be to communicate with someone displaying the opposite body language to you?

Our previous telephone scenario will have given you clues as to how to use verbal matching and mirroring when you are coaching a coachee over the phone and you have never met her. You still have many clues about her body language but you rely on your ears not your eyes to read them.

Listen to the tone of voice your coachee uses. Is she calm, angry, hesitant, unsure, focused, confident, excited? Listening to her vocal cues will tell you as much as her facial expression would if you were sitting opposite her. A coachee who suddenly sees a way forward will talk faster and more loudly, for instance, than when she feels stuck. When she makes a decision about what to do next, her voice will sound stronger, more committed. If she is angry, her voice may get higher in pitch and then deepen as she calms down. When she is thinking through a problem her tone and the speed and pitch at which she talks will all reflect her thought processes. Where she is silent or where she can't get her words out fast enough, are all auditory clues for you to pick up on, as is a sigh or hesitation before she answers a question. So listen for the tone, pitch, speed, volume and fluency of your coachee's speech to understand how to match her vocal body language, and check your own while you are at it. According to Moir and Jessel (1998: 17), when the sexes are compared, women show a greater sensitivity to sound. The dripping tap will get a woman out of bed before the man has even woken up. Six times as many girls as boys can sing in tune.

The point of vocal and physical matching and mirroring is not only as a tool to let your coachee know you understand her perspective; it is also a means to help guide her to a productive place where solutions and strategy are accessible. You do this by subtly shifting *your* tone, body language and mood – such as sitting back in your chair (if you've been matching your coachee by sitting on the edge), by slowing your speech down (if you've been keeping up with your coachee's quick pace) – thereby guiding them along. If they don't follow, it is too soon, so go back to their 'state' for a few more minutes and try again. The idea of guiding is so that the main part of the coaching session can be productive. If a coachee is very upset, frustrated or cross, however clever, open or wise to your questioning, you could be met with one word answers and an unwillingness to move forwards. This is why getting your body and vocal language into sync with theirs at the beginning of the session is critical.

Over the telephone, you would do the same verbally. You might even provide a vocal 'break' in the session. This would be useful when you've heard their description of their situation, but before you go on to the G of the TGROW model you would take an audible breath, brighten your voice and say something like:

▍ **'OK, so tell me how you'd most like to use this session today?'**

It is the same question we suggested when dealing with negativity, but it is worth repeating because it is so powerful. This question vocalised in your brighter voice will help signify to the coachee an intention for positive change. Try practising these techniques on your friends and family and take notice of how they open up to you, whether they talk more, if the conversation is taken to a deeper level or if, just by your complete 'being in the moment' with them, they sense your interest and presence.

2 Matching mood versus matching energy

When we teach this to students we always get asked, 'What if someone comes into a coaching session feeling angry or disappointed or frustrated – how do you match that?' The answer is: you match the energy the coachee is displaying, not the mood. For instance, someone who is frustrated – let's say about traffic jams on the way to a session – may walk into your room with arms flailing, talking quickly, ranting about the roads and so on. The coach would match their energy by using the same speed or volume of voice and using their arms or hands animatedly – it is something you might do naturally with a friend or relative. But you don't need to match their mood and end up as frustrated as they are about the state of the roads! However, by matching her energy and then calming your own energy – perhaps by taking a deep breath and smiling or showing her to her seat – you will be able to break that state of mind and bring some focus to the session. The idea isn't to bring the coach down but to move the coachee to a productive state.

3 Making eye contact

Not everyone makes eye contact, which is a shame as it is such a true reflection of how someone feels. Eye contact, like body language, can say infinitely more than words. People avoid it for all kinds of reasons though: some don't want to be seen, others feel invisible and so they reflect that back to those around them by almost making themselves invisible by avoiding eye contact. Others are lying and know that their rapid eye movements and insincerity will give them away. Others are just shy. Next time you go to the supermarket or walk the dog, take a look around you and see how many people actually make eye contact with each other. We've observed cashiers at supermarket tills put their customer's shopping through the till, ask for the money, do the financial transaction and give them a receipt, all without making eye contact – it is mad when you think about it!

However, for some people it just feels unnatural – not everyone is confident about looking at someone else directly – and we mustn't forget that sometimes it isn't socially acceptable (e.g. on tubes and buses). But in a coaching session it is entirely appropriate. Eye contact is linked to emotional response, it is linked to people having a unique relationship with each other and, of course, women are very visual – which brings into place Key Principles 1, 4 and 5 without even blinking. For a woman, it is intensely productive and necessary to make eye contact with the person she is talking to confidentially – it proves to her that you are listening, that you 'get' her, that you are with her.

So what about telephone sessions? Can it work without eye contact? Most definitely yes. Not making eye contact with your coachee when you are physically together is making a negative statement, but over the phone she isn't expecting eye contact so she isn't affected by not having it. Alternatively you use the tone of your voice as well as interjections, such as 'Ah', 'Mmm', 'Ahuh', 'Right', 'OK' and 'Yes', to reassure her that you are there, listening and really understanding her. We regularly coach long distance international coachees very effectively and we never meet them. There is something about being a familiar voice over the phone – and yet knowing that you won't ever bump into that person in the street, that they will never meet your friends and family – that safeguards confidentiality like nothing else.

4 Nodding

Nodding, smiling and using facial expressions to let your coachee know you are taking in everything she says is another ingredient to building rapport quickly. We already know that a coach shouldn't be judgemental, give his or her advice, or pass comment on whether they think their coachee's plan will work or not. But we are human, and your coachee wants to talk to a human being, not a computer. As time goes on you will become skilled in how to interact with your coachee honestly while not passing judgement on the content of the session. What you are aiming for with your facial expressions is a connection – for your coachee to know that you can see her perspective and that you are genuinely interested in her take on her situation. Your nods, smiles and expressions will let her know that you have complete and unwavering confidence that she will make the right choices to bring balance back into her situation, as will the reassuring, affirming noises and words you make when coaching over the phone. This intervention is intensely powerful for a woman, so never underestimate the power of your attention.

We gave the example above of a woman acting as if she was confident and consciously using her body language as a mask to hide her true feelings. Well, in positive circumstances 'acting as if …' can be a remarkable tool for change. Shakespeare gave the excellent advice, 'Assume a virtue if you have it not … For use can change the stamp of nature' (*Hamlet*, III, 3). Deliberately behaving as though you are the person you want to be can help you to take on the positive attributes of that person. Many actors studying a role will use their character's posture, gait, mannerisms, tone of voice and so on, to help them to understand and become that character. This works for a coachee when she is moving towards her dream, something she dearly wants and desires. It is only when using this method to cover up or suppress true emotions, fragility or sadness that it is potentially damaging.

Life coach Anthony Robbins says, 'Years ago one of the most important ways I changed my life was to change the pattern of the way I moved, the way I gestured, the way I spoke ... My movements were simply copies of what I had seen other extremely confident people do. All I did was to mimic them' (2001: 64). He explains that consciously copying in this way began to change the way he thought and felt, until he wasn't acting any more but had genuinely become more confident.

Getting your coachee to notice her body language can give her options to change a situation. One coachee, for instance, talked about how intimidated she felt by the behaviour of a colleague. She described feeling as though this person was constantly invading her space, not giving her time to think and deliberately getting in her way. One example she gave was a clash over a room booking. Both our coachee and her colleague were scheduled to teach students in the same room at the same time and although she arrived in the room first, she had been the one forced out. The same situation was about to be repeated as the timetable hadn't been changed, so it was a fitting topic for her session, which went like this:

COACH: Where are you when your colleague arrives in the room?

COACHEE: I'm sitting at the desk.

COACH: Tell me more about how you're sitting.

COACHEE: Well, I suppose I'm leaning on the desk for support with my shoulders nearly touching my ears because I'm dreading the confrontation coming my way.

COACH: What about your feet?

COACHEE: Well, because I'm tense my knees are drawn up touching the underneath of the desk so only the front part of my feet are touching the floor, as though I'm on tiptoe.

COACH: If you saw yourself in the position you've described what would it tell you?

COACHEE: That I'm scared of being attacked and I'm trying to hold on to my space, which is true, but not how I want X to see the situation.

COACH: What could you do differently so that X gets a different message?

COACHEE: I could change my body language to say I have a right to stay put and that they should leave instead. I'd sit back in my chair with my feet planted on the floor and my hands on the desk and my shoulders relaxed and hold my head up high. That would feel better, but surely changing the way I sit can't influence a bully, can it?

Please note that the coach wasn't trying to get her to see anything in particular; instead, they were asking questions to get the coachee thinking about her body language.

The coachee got her own answer. She did change her body language and her colleague, sensing that she meant business, withdrew from the room and let her have it after all. She continued to ensure that her body language gave the messages she wanted and her colleague gave her more space and less aggravation.

So whether you use it to achieve a superb rapport with your coachee or to help her raise her self esteem and confidence, you can see that being very aware of how body language affects us is a core skill for a coach.

8   Communication Skills With a Feminine Edge

Men and women communicate differently. It is one of the most fundamental differences between us, which means that if you are going to become a successful expert in coaching women, you will need to have a deep understanding of those differences. But before we start, let's be clear about exactly what we are saying here.

Men and women have a tendency to behave, think and communicate using different language, inference and meaning, although none of us are restricted to a particular mode of communication. As Simma Leiberman states in her article 'Differences in Male and Female Communication Styles':

> While much has been said about women and men being from different planets and having their own cultures, the reality is that we have all grown up on the same planet, and interact with each other in different ways on a daily basis.
>
> It is good fun to look at communication differences between men and women but we also have to be careful not to assume that all men will act in a certain way and all women act in another way. We are on a continuum: there are women who have some traits that might be attributed to the archetypal 'male' style and there are times when it is necessary to use this mode; the same applies to men. Here are two examples ...
>
> 1   The head surgeon in an operating room is a woman. If she is operating on you would you prefer she uses a consensus based style to make decisions and ask everyone what they think during the operation, or a hierarchical style and tell the medical personnel when to sew you up. The consensus based style is considered female and the hierarchical is considered male, but for that woman to be the head surgeon, you can be sure that she had

to get comfortable giving orders and having them obeyed in the operating room.

2   The executive director of your organization is male. The majority of the staff is female. You are all going on a team building retreat, but the destination has not been decided yet. Would you rather have a director who decides for the group where to go, even if the whole organization hates it, or would you rather he takes a consensus based approach and asks for input? Consensus decision making style is considered a female style, but if that executive director is serious about team building he'd better ask people for ideas or they might decide they aren't comfortable with his choice and be resentful, not the environment to build a successful work team.

Whether it is nature or nurture we recognise, there will be some individuals who possess almost none of the traits attributed to their gender. They may have been teased, harassed or excluded from groups and events because of this, which is why it is important to understand male and female cultural norms, but also to recognise that many people don't fit the standard mould.

So what exactly are those communication differences? We think there are three distinct areas:

1   A woman's primary response is often an emotional one.
2   Women need to know (and expect) that they have a unique connection with others.
3   Women listen very well by nature and have an in-built need to hear their own words.

Let's look at those differences in a little more depth.

1 A woman's primary response is often an emotional one

We spoke to Juliet Price, Managing Director of HR Management and Health & Safety firm Park City (www.parkcity.co.uk), and she highlighted what we consider to be the most important communication difference – that women attach emotion to their thoughts and behaviour in the first instance, whereas men's initial responses to situations are generally more unemotional. Men will see a situation and go into 'solutions mode' whereas women will see situations for how it makes them feel, and look for solutions only after they've explored their emotional reactions. Typically their emotional state can influence their thinking and reactions. On the whole, Juliet finds that the women she deals with in leadership positions are successful leaders because of this emotional first response. In her experience, these women have a high degree of 'emotional intelligence' which means they can work on the perhaps male dominated solutions approach and couple that with an emotional understanding of where everyone involved will be coming from. These women deal successfully with both the best solution and the emotional fall-out for all involved. It is that multifaceted approach that you will become familiar with the longer you coach women. Women are just more likely to demonstrate first Key Principle 4 – that women are emotionally literate and so are willing to acknowledge, explore and express emotions. As Michele Alexander and Wendy Wood observe: 'the typical woman in our society is believed to be more emotionally expressive, concerned with her own and others' feeling states and emotionally labile than the typical man' (2000: 192).

So, if one of the main communication strategies women employ is to consider their emotional response to a situation before a practical solution based thought process can be considered, what does that mean for a coach? It means that there are potentially two pitfalls:

1 The coach could get too caught up in the coachee's initial emotional response to help the coachee reach the next stage of finding solutions.

2 If the coach isn't expecting an emotional response they may feel uncomfortable and rush too quickly to the solutions stage before the coachee has had the chance to properly clarify and process their feelings towards their situation.

First of all, let's look at the first pitfall in progress, in which the coach gets too caught up in the coachee's emotional response to be able to move her forwards.

> *Topic: Coachee needs to move house*
>
> *Goal: To explore some criteria that the new area would need to have*

COACH: So, if you were to move house, where would you most love to move to?

COACHEE: Well, that's the problem, I don't really know. I mean, moving is the best thing for my family. We've outgrown the house we're in and we don't need to stay in this area. The girls are coming up to leaving school, so technically we could go anywhere … it's just that leaving the house … if we could pick it up and take it with us that would be perfect!

COACH: *(smiling)* Really? Would you love to do that?

COACHEE: Ah absolutely! Do you know, we've lived in that house for over twenty years! In fact, one of my daughters was born there. We built most of it too … when we first moved in it was tiny. We always saw the potential in extending. That house has so many memories, it's going to be such a wrench to leave it. We need to move for necessity now though. I just don't know how I'm going to bring myself to pack up this house and even look for another one! I don't think any other house (or area for that matter) is going to come up to the same standards as what we have already. We do need to move but it's not going to be easy.

COACH: I can see that this is a really hard decision you've had to make, you really don't want to actually move do you?

COACHEE: No … not at all! Every time I walk into the main high street, I see my daughter in my mind's eye coming out of the newsagents doing her paper round when she was 15. She hated that paper round! She didn't like getting up early, but she did it because she wanted to go on a school skiing trip. We told her if she wanted to go, she'd have to pay for some of it. *(laughs)*

COACH: It sounds like you laid down some really great ethics there.

COACHEE: Well, we tried, we thought that was important. Now my other daughter, she wasn't at all like that. I remember when she started a school project, she organised all her friends to do the work – they had to set up a stall in the square and sell cookies. She came home early because they were doing all the work – I even baked all the cookies!

Do you see how this dialogue seems like two friends meeting and one explaining about her past and the other one listening? There is absolutely no sense of coaching here at all. The coach has got caught up in the emotions of her coachee's story and, so far, we've heard three family history stories and no mention of the goal itself, which was to explore some criteria that the new area would need to have. The coach is interested and engaged but sounds more like a new friend instead of a professional.

Now here is an example of pitfall number two in progress, where the coach isn't addressing her coachee's emotional needs at all and is trying to push her forward towards a solution too quickly:

> COACH: So, if you were to move house, where would you most love to move to?
>
> COACHEE: Well, that's the problem, I don't really know. I mean, moving is the best thing for my family. We've outgrown the house we're in and we don't need to stay in this area. The girls are coming up to leaving school, so technically we could go anywhere … it's just that leaving the house … if we could pick it up and take it with us that would be perfect!
>
> COACH: So, you don't need to stay in this area?
>
> COACHEE: No.
>
> COACH: What would you be looking for particularly in the area you decide to settle in?
>
> COACHEE: I hadn't really thought about it. This house has been such a part of our family lives for so many years. You know we built half of it, when we bought it it was tiny! One of my daughters was born at home too, did I tell you that? And both the girls went to the primary school up the road. Wherever we turn in this village, there are memories … so I haven't really thought about what I'd look for in a new area.
>
> COACH: If you chose three things that were most important to you about the new area what would they be?
>
> COACHEE: *(silence)* I have no idea!

In this example, the coachee isn't getting anywhere fast. Technically there's nothing wrong with the coach's questions at all. The first question is open and exploratory, the second question is closed but it is a clarification question so that is fine, the third and fourth questions are good open, probing questions. But what the coach has failed to do is to recognise and acknowledge her coachee's emotional response to the need to move. Women do need to feel properly heard and listened to. We've already ascertained that coaching isn't a firing off of sensible questions one after another and that, although you are working through the TGROW model, you are still actively engaging with another person, someone who needs to feel valued, listened to and to have the room to explore her feelings.

Now look at this example, in which the coach acknowledges the coachee's emotional response but is also able to move her forward positively:

COACH: So, if you were to move house, where would you most love to move to?

COACHEE: Well, that's the problem, I don't really know. I mean, moving is the best thing for my family. We've outgrown the house we're in and we don't need to stay in this area. The girls are coming up to leaving school, so technically we could go anywhere ... it's just that leaving the house ... if we could pick it up and take it with us that would be perfect!

COACH: (smiling) Really? Would you love to do that?

COACHEE: Ah absolutely! Do you know, we've lived in that house for over twenty years! In fact, one of my daughters was born there. We built most of it too ... when we first moved in it was tiny. We always saw the potential in extending. That house has so many memories, it's going to be such a wrench to leave it. We need to move for necessity now though. I just don't know how I'm going to bring myself to pack up this house and even look for another one! I don't think any other house (or area for that matter) is going to come up to the same standards as what we have already. We do need to move but it's not going to be easy.

COACH: There are a lot of memories for you in this house aren't there?

COACHEE: Everywhere! I have such strong memories of everything that happened in this house and also in the village. We've been here such a long time, it's really difficult to even think about moving actually.

COACH: I can see that … *(silence, mirroring coachee's body language)* When we started this session, we talked about the goal for today being to explore some criteria that the new area would need to have. Can I check at this point if that is the very best use of this session for you today?

COACHEE: Yes, it is. Honestly, I just hadn't really realised how emotional this move was going to be, but it does need to happen. So yes, thanks for checking, but what would be most productive would be to talk about the new area and the criteria it needs to have. Having that will make this easier I think.

COACH: OK.

Can you see the difference? The coach's first question is enquiring and open, the second question is engaging and picking up with enthusiasm on her coachee's comment, but it is the third question that is so powerful. It acknowledges the coachee's memories of this house and she is telling her that she can see this is a difficult topic for her. The coachee's answer to that question allows her to hear her own words, to self acknowledge her emotional attachment to the house and the village. The coach's next question is perfect at this juncture. She is basically saying, 'Now we've recognised that this is such an emotional topic, can I check that the goal is the right one for you today?' – the coach is bringing the coachee back to the goal for the session respectfully but purposefully. She is not allowing her to wander in and around family stories, but simply acknowledging that there must be a huge history to this topic and checking that the practical 'finding criteria' goal they started with really is the best use of her time. She is asking her permission, she is checking in, she is clarifying.

The coachee's next answer brings into play the third communication difference that we think is vital to understand in order to communicate with a woman – that women listen very well by nature (on which more below), so let her listen to herself and hear her own words. By the coach acknowledging her coachee's emotions, the coachee was able to hear her own words and hadn't realised until that point just how difficult this move would be. However, she then decided that the practical approach would be the best use of her time in the session and that having a sound solution could make the situation a little easier. The coach then respects that decision without any judgement or intonation about which way she thinks the coachee should approach this topic.

By reflecting on these scenarios you can see how it is not just the question you ask or the intonation that you ask it with, but it is taking into account all three of a woman's communication styles.

Let's move onto the second communication style.

2 Women need to know (and expect) a unique connection with others

When a woman divulges information about herself to anyone, she will feel as though her connection with that person is very special. When she employs a coach, she is trusting you enough to open up and explain the in's and out's of her life to a virtual stranger because of your professional standing. If you forget Key Principle 1 – that women want to feel their relationship with their coach is unique and different from the coach's relationship to other coachees – your coachee will start to feel very uncomfortable about the information she is giving you. This principle is not there for vanity purposes or to 'fool' the coachee into thinking she is your only coachee. She knows you are a professional and of course you will have other coachees, but what she will expect is that having confided in you, your relationship with her will be different from your other coachees. An excellent coach will take this to heart and understand how to make each relationship unique to each coachee.

If you are wondering what it would take for you to do that, consider the relationships you have now. Do you have brothers and sisters? You probably have a different relationship with each sibling and a special but different connection to them both. It is the same with parents of more than one child. You form a special and unique relationship with each child based on their personalities, the types of conversations you have and the things you do together. Those with more than one pet for instance will also be able to tell you how each animal responds differently to you, and it is the same with acquaintances. Most of us have friends who we interact with differently, who appreciate us for our different qualities, so your relationship with your coachees as unique individuals will work in the same way: always unique.

3 Women listen very well by nature and have an in-built need to hear their own words

What is going to set you apart from coaches who haven't been trained to coach women is that you have learned the true power of letting a woman listen to herself. We so rarely get to listen to our own words. It is an odd thing to say because we hear what we are saying all the time, but the difference in a coaching session is that no one is there to contradict you, no one is going to have another funnier, cleverer or more interesting story to tell, no one is going to tell you what to do or how to handle yourself. When we don't have those normal interruptions we hear ourselves in a completely different way. We've already seen in the dialogue above where our coachee was talking about moving house, that the coach let her hear her own words and she realised just how difficult moving was going to be. This happens every day when you work as a coach for women.

9 A Woman's Reputation With Herself

Self esteem: the reputation one has with oneself.

This definition of self esteem is one we heard from a psychiatrist being interviewed on the radio one Sunday morning a few years ago. It seemed to sum up exactly what it meant for us. We've also heard some excellent definitions from our coaching students over the years. One in particular was from Razwana Wahid, who referred to self esteem as 'the level to which I respect myself'. Whatever your definition, one thing is for sure: self esteem is a hard thing to measure. It is invisible but felt; it is intangible but definitely there; it has a presence that a whole room can see yet has no definable shape or form. It is powerful enough to literally make or break a woman's life and, as a coach, your questions are capable of locating it, defining it, giving it shape, and making it tangible. With the right intonation, the perfect level of enquiry and a genuine desire *not* to fix it for your coachee, you can be part of a process that builds a woman's self esteem which will enable her to achieve everything she has always wanted, and probably more.

We spoke to Geraldine Steele about her self esteem journey. Her story illustrates so clearly how a strong and successful woman battled with low self esteem and how it can be overcome and won. 'Battling self esteem on your own', she says 'is a very lonely place, it's like having a monster with you.' Geraldine went from being a businesswoman and nightclub owner – a well known and revered figure and part of her community whose opinion was valued and sought – to being the exact opposite of all of those things.

> It happened overnight when my thirty-four-year-old marriage broke up. My self esteem disappeared very quickly, I changed my whole life. I stayed indoors, shut the curtains, didn't see anyone for days. I refused to answer the telephone. I hid away and my thought patterns were very negative. I reduced any previous success or standing I'd had in my mind to nothing. My mind had a way of making my future look

very bleak plus it made looking back on previously successful times extremely painful as it tainted happy memories with negativity too. A low self esteem can be extremely damaging and can affect every part of a woman's life. I lost my sense of self and my sense of a future.

The turning point for Geraldine was a fleeting thought that entered her head: 'I can't do this any more.' She continued:

> I think I scared myself with how low I'd really allowed myself to get. It was like an electric shock and what frightened me more was how comfortable that place was becoming. I decided I needed to pull myself back up. It took a good while and plenty of baby steps – coaching was one of those baby steps.

A woman's self esteem comes in all shapes and sizes and Geraldine's, as you can see, was a severe case. Regardless of how low a woman has got before she realises she deserves more, no matter how low she believes her self esteem to be and no matter how it has affected her life, the common denominator for women who seek coaching for low self esteem is that they have all realised that something needs to change, that it is time to find another way of working – they all want something different and they are all ready to move forwards. Without that *will* to want to change, coaching cannot and will not be of any benefit. Your coachee is the only person truly responsible for her own thought patterns, behaviour and comfort zones. When your coachee wants to change, she will find you; and Geraldine not only found coaching itself but our coaching diploma too. Now a qualified coach working within an organisation, she runs self esteem and motivation courses.

As you can see from Geraldine's story, for a woman self esteem is linked directly to her success or failure. Success as she perceives it, in her own mind, not what everyone else sees. It is entirely possible for a woman to be outwardly seen by her friends, family and colleagues as a successful woman, but if she doesn't believe it or see it that way, she won't be living as confidently or as fully as her friends presume. A woman's self esteem is what frames her capabilities. If a woman feels capable of doing something well, if her self esteem is strong, then she will feel able to overcome anything. If she loses confidence in her capabilities, if her reputation with herself is damaged, she will have no belief that she is capable of living a future that is any different to her past. For us, that has been the biggest fundamental difference to many of our coachees; they realise that just because their past has been one way, it doesn't mean their future will be the same.

We asked Gabrielle Blackman-Sheppard, author and coach with almost twenty years experience of coaching men, if she thought self esteem affected her male coachees in a similar way to our female coachees. This is what she said:

> To a man, self-esteem is linked to his ranking amongst other men. He tends to ask himself 'What makes me a man?' or 'What makes me a successful man?' Competitive positioning is extremely important (certainly to start with) although there are some men who refuse to play that game. Very early on, those men decide they won't enter the competitive race. They don't feel the need to put themselves in a position of competition. Rather they make their own way and refuse to measure themselves against another men's success. For the so-called alpha male though, self esteem is about where they think they fit 'in the pack'. It is about the reputation they have with their peers, not the idea they have of themselves. Their mates, other male co-workers, professional acquaintances and so on, all aspire to fit in their different packs. Reputation, power, wealth, standing, ego and stature all play a part. Once men know where they fit and have built a reputation in their environment, they can acquire a superior level of maturity and be able to let go of all that hierarchy. They make peace with themselves as the men they are inside. This level of maturity by the way has very little to do with age. For instance an older man with 75-year-old wrinkles and a 25-year-old woman on his arm still feels the need to maintain his place in the pack, whereas a much younger man may be capable of opting out of that competitive race for a more contemplative or creative life, knowing it is the right decision for him. Let us not forget that although this behaviour is typically male, there are also alpha females in this world, keen to link their self esteem to status and ranking within a social or professional group. For both men and women, there can also be what some describe as a 'moment of clarity' once they have reached their perceived 'successful' level or status when they think, 'Is this all there is?', 'What now?', 'Am I missing something?' or even 'Do I deserve to be here after all?' It is typically at this point that coaching can be of most value in

helping people to realign values and beliefs which, yes, women will tend to address as their self esteem whereas men will be more likely to address as 'What else can I achieve?', 'Where else can I take my skills and experience?', 'Where else can I be successful?'

Gabrielle's opinion is echoed by Moir and Jessel in their book *Brainsex*: 'Self esteem is equally important to men and women, but studies conclude that levels of self esteem in men and women are affected by different things: by "affiliative success" in women – that is the depth and strength of their relationships – but by "occupational success" in men' (1998: 166).

What causes low self esteem? Our experiences as a child and as an adult shape how we rate ourselves. Self esteem is decreased by our being criticised, put down or compared unfavourably to others, being neglected or rejected, having our fears or opinions ignored, being turned down for a job or made redundant, or seeing unachievable ideals in the media. These all sink into our unconscious and, if we let them, can have a destructive impact.

So how do we start to coach a woman with low self esteem? We hope you know by now that walking into a coaching session with a prescriptive, 'Yes, I think your self esteem has suffered a lot, let's see what we can do about that' is strictly off limits. But your female coachee is very likely to describe her self esteem to you and to talk about it openly.

For a new coach the possibility of having an impact on someone's self esteem can feel overwhelming. However, don't forget that self esteem is simply the reputation we have with ourselves. Much like the chapter on negotiating negativity, a woman's reputation with herself needs to be taken seriously and if you do so she will thank you for taking the time to help her recognise it, explore it and work on it. What she most wants from you is to communicate and to learn through that interaction. Keep Key Principle 2 to the fore: women learn best through discussion and have highly developed verbal skills. Let her talk about it and discuss it, because you might be the only one in her life giving her that opportunity. What she won't thank you for is glossing over it, being scared of its existence or being too self conscious to go there with her.

Coaching gives a woman choices about how to work through her issues on self esteem, and your questions and manner will support that process. You are not changing her self esteem for her, you are not directing her or pointing her in the direction of a more fulfilled self esteem; it is not your responsibility to 'build her up'. Your reputation as a coach is not on the line. Quite the opposite, the spotlight is on the coachee, and if she has come to the same conclusion that Geraldine did – that with baby steps she needs to change her inner reputation – then your being there and your support will be exactly what she needs.

So, if we are going to help you take your coachee's reputation with herself seriously, and her conversations with you are going to be different from those she has with her friends, what kind of questions could be helpful? Well, first of all, remember the TGROW model. Make sure that the *topic* and *goal* for the session are clear. If your coachee identifies her self esteem as an important priority in getting to the goal for the session, then it will be entirely appropriate for you to work on it. If not, respect her opinion – she knows best.

How will you know if self esteem issues are getting in the way for your coachee? You will hear statements like:

> **'I couldn't do that/see myself doing that.'**
>
> **'I'm not the sort of person who can ...'**
>
> **'I've never been able to ...'**

One way to work with your coachee to change these kinds of negative statements would be to talk about belief systems (more about this later), but even without mentioning belief systems your conversation could go something like this:

COACHEE: I'd really like to get a qualification in something, to have letters after my name and a diploma to put on the wall, but I couldn't see myself doing that.

COACH: What is it about that idea that makes you think you couldn't do it?

COACHEE: Well, I've always had pretty low self esteem. I got told too often at school that I was untidy and too slow to pick things up.

COACH: Would it be helpful talk more about your self esteem?

It is a closed question, but she has already brought up the topic of self esteem so it is fine to ask if she would like to talk about it.

If the answer is yes then you can go ahead. You could play with Key Principle 5 – women are able to use visualisation very effectively – to find out exactly what shape your coachee thinks her self esteem is in. You can ask directly:

> **'What shape is your self esteem?'**
>
> **'If it was a colour what colour would it be now?'**
>
> **'What colour would it need to be to move you closer towards your goal?'**
>
> **'If it was an animal what would it be?'**
>
> **'What animal would it need to be to start making a positive impact on your life?'**
>
> **'How strong is your self esteem right now?'**
>
> **'What could you achieve if it was a little stronger?'**
>
> **'What could you achieve if it was a lot stronger?'**
>
> **'When did you last feel a strong self esteem?'**
>
> **'What do people with strong self esteem act or look like?'**

These are all valid questions – they are open, enquiring, information gathering and they place no judgement on how self esteem *should* look or feel. What these questions do is give your coachee complete freedom to tell you exactly what she feels in her own words and using her own terminology. The information you get from her answers will help you to formulate your next question and will mean you can reflect her own language back to her.

Let's take an example of a woman who uses visualisation as her dominant method of communication:

COACH: Tell me a bit more about what your self esteem looks like?

COACHEE: Well ... it's small and round, a bit like the moon at night – about that size. It looks a very long way away. It's quite bright but the glare doesn't light up much around it, only a few inches.

COACH: What impact does its size have on its effectiveness?

COACHEE: Well, it's not very effective that size. It would need to be a bit bigger to be effective, but most of all it would need to be brighter. In fact, if it was brighter it would make more of an impact. It would light up more around it – if it was more sun-like and less moon-like it would have a larger sphere around it – that would feel good. Turning it into sunshine would feel lovely.

COACH: If it was more sunshine-like how would that impact on your goal for today's session?

COACHEE: I'd have more options I think. If the sun's rays were brighter, it would shine further afield, so I'd see things that are in the dark at the moment.

COACH: How would you go about changing it from a moon to a sun?

COACHEE: Well, I'd just have to tell myself it's daytime and not night time! I think I've been living like it's night time but nothing much happens at night ... I need to be in the daytime to be really effective now. I'll concentrate on that.

That is a short excerpt of a coaching session that actually took place. It is helpful to illustrate how playing with the images your coachee presents you with can have such a direct impact on how she changes her own perceptions. The lessons learnt above stayed with this particular coachee for a long time and enabled her to grow her business, which is what she wanted.

We've spoken above about your coachee's preferred mode of communication (i.e. whether they are visual, auditory or kinaesthetic), in its most basic sense and you can use this information.

If you've noticed that your coachee is kinaesthetic, these questions could feel appropriate:

> **'What does your self esteem feel like?'**
>
> **'What would an uncrushable self esteem feel like?'**
>
> **'How would you feel different with a strong sense of self?'**
>
> **'If you could touch it, what temperature would it be?'**
>
> **'If it was material, what would it feel like?'**
>
> **'Where in your body do you feel it?'**

If you've noticed they are visual, these questions could look interesting:

> **'If you could picture your self esteem, what would it look like?'**
>
> **'What shape is your self esteem right now?'**
>
> **'How do you see your self esteem?'**
>
> **'What do you think your self esteem looks like to other people?'**
>
> **'What colour is your self esteem?'**
>
> **'If your self esteem was strong, what would it look like?'**

If you've noticed they are auditory, these questions will ring a bell for them:

> **'If your self esteem could talk, what would it say?'**
>
> **'What kind of voice does your self esteem have?'**
>
> **'What kind of voice you would like to give it instead?'**
>
> **'If it sounded stronger, what would it sound like?'**
>
> **'If your self esteem was a noise, what would it be?'**
>
> **'How loud is your self esteem?'**

Please do note that there is much more to a person's preferred mode of communication than the above and there are many books which will explain this in vast detail and which you might find helpful. For coaching purposes though, to be aware of its existence at a basic level will be of value. By now you will be flicking between the GRO and W aspects of the TGROW model, you will have a heightened awareness of working with Key Principles 1–6 and your coachee will know you are on her wavelength – that she doesn't have to be anything other than herself and you will be working together in the best way for her. She will be fixing problems, moving forward, learning about herself and understanding the power of her mind and thoughts.

As part of this process you will also be making her intrinsically aware of her comfort zones. We mention this now because comfort zones are so closely linked to self esteem. Remember how Geraldine described her lowest moments? She said 'what frightened me more was how comfortable that place was becoming'. Low self esteem in a woman leads to lower self confidence, which leads to an unwillingness to try new things, which leads to repeatedly doing things you are comfortable with, which means restricting where you go, what you do and ultimately how you perceive your capabilities. Typically we describe comfort zones as the activities we feel able to do without pushing ourselves at all. Some people regularly trek to the deepest, darkest places on earth and call it adventure, while someone else's view of adventure is driving on a major motorway. Never assume that you know where your coachee's comfort zones are and never assume they are going to be happy to consider crossing those self made boundaries, even for their own self development.

While one woman will find discovering where she naturally stops moving forwards as intriguing, a learning experience even, another will find it very limiting and daunting. Her reaction to those self made boundaries will need your kid gloves and sensitive questioning. Have the same conversation with your next coachee, however, and she may realise to her horror how much her self imposed comfort zones have impacted on her life and be determined to find a way to push herself forward. These women will work hard to change those barriers. Other women will be very reluctant to move from their comfort zones, even though they realise how restricting they may have become. Geraldine did move beyond her comfort zones. She noticed an advert for the coaching diploma course with us, and even though it scared her, even though she had no real idea if she could even do it, she pushed ahead anyway. She knew that it was what she needed to do and it paid off for her.

Know this: it is not your place to push your coachee to move her comfort zones for the greater good. If your coachee is resisting moving forwards, ask her how that impacts on her goal for the session. Check if her goal needs to change. Ask her what her motivation to moving past those barriers would be – what is her drive? We've known coachees move forwards with a goal, despite understanding that they are working within self imposed restrictions. Sometimes it is the comfort zones *within* the comfort zones that need to move first before major change can take place. Let her go at her own pace and she will move. Push her and the chances are she will keep stubbornly rooted to the spot and tell her friends that coaching doesn't work. It is all about a series of steps to get from one place to another – one coachee will make it in four, another in forty-four. To presume anything around this very delicate area will turn your female coachee off instantly and she will cancel her next session with you – her trust in you will have gone along with her plummeting self esteem. Instead, what you are after here is a real reason for change, her emotional buy-in, a reason that is good enough to see your coachee through her darkest days, when you are not around and the memories and energy of your coaching session seem a dim and distant vibe – that is when she will continue to push through uncomfortable phases in her life and when her reputation as 'a woman who can' will find its voice. She will find within herself her deepest strength and self reliance. Every woman has a core strength from which to draw on – finding it and feeling it will impact her for the rest of her life.

Remember also what you learnt about going to 'la-la land'. If your coachee does want to work on going beyond her comfort zones, ask those 'If anything is possible ... ' type questions to free her up from the habitual limits she sets for herself. You could ask:

> **'If there really was no limit to what you could accomplish, what would you consider?'**
>
> **'If you could create a whole new range of opportunities what would they be?'**
>
> **'If your self image could be anything you want what would it be?'**

So, what have you learnt so far about coaching a woman with self esteem issues?

- To be directed by your coachee and not try to 'solve' her self esteem problems.

- To listen to her and to take her reputation with herself seriously.

- To explore the connection between her goal for the session and her self esteem.

- To help give this intangible energy some form or shape in order to gain clarity and movement.

- To respect that comfort zones are all wrapped up in the same delicate tissue paper as self esteem itself.

- To work with your coachee's comfort zones as she understands them, not with your perceptions of where they should be.

- To identify a real reason for change.

Even if a woman's past hasn't been the life she would have loved, it is still the life she actually lived. It is reality and, therefore, it is the comfort zone that she knows well. To take that away from her will not win you any favours. To let her explore it, feel it, define it, touch it – that is true exploration and, for a woman, it is also true growth.

10 The Wheel of a Woman's Life

By now, you will be very aware of the complexity, speed and flexibility of a woman's mind and will have started to understand how to ethically help your female coachees sift through their thoughts and get inside any chaotic or confusing topics. You will also have an understanding of how the TGROW model can help unravel virtually any tangled web (as long as the coachee has a genuine desire to disentangle it, that is). When coachees come presenting clear topics with easy-to-articulate goals, student coaches feel very much in their comfort zone; the TGROW model and the inclusion of the six key principles to coaching a woman will work together seamlessly. But a student or an inexperienced coach's confidence can be rocked if your coachee is confused or has little idea where to begin. If every area of your coachee's life seems to be affected with stress and uncertainty, where do you start? With no definable topic, how do you tease one out?

In earlier chapters we identified ways to help coachees find those areas which make real and measurable differences. Now we will introduce you to another tool, the wheel of life. It is perfect for the way a woman's mind works because of its visual impact (remember Key Principle 5, that women are very visual) and it kick-starts discussion around the topics of her life (which incorporates Key Principle 2, that women learn best through discussion and have highly developed verbal skills). So, for a woman who isn't sure what to focus on first, the wheel of life is a really helpful way of identifying which areas of her life are working well and which need attention; in short, where to start and what her priorities are.

So what exactly is a wheel of life? Essentially, it is a circle, generally with eight spokes, each of which is labelled with a key area of the coachee's life.

The typical basic wheel looks like this:

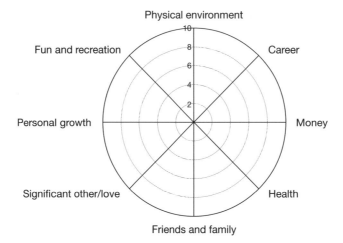

This covers the most significant areas of life, so you could choose to start with those areas. Using this, your coachee can see in front of her a map of her life – on paper, in black and white. If you are coaching over the phone, talk your coachee through drawing it for herself. Transcribe it along with her so you can keep track of what she is seeing. You could work with your coachee and ask which areas she would like to see on there. Our example is just that, an example. Here is what to do next:

Step 1

Explain that each spoke of the wheel represents an area of her life which is measured on a scale of 0–10, with 0 being at the centre of the wheel and 10 on the rim of the wheel. 0 means that her satisfaction with that area is very low and 10 means that she is completely happy with that area of her life.

Step 2

Ask her what score she would put on each spoke of the wheel on the scale of 0–10 and to rank all areas of the wheel. If your coachee finds it difficult to score each spoke, firstly assure her that it is essential to be honest. The wheel isn't about having a perfect set of 10's; it is about having a tool to help identify which parts of her life need her attention. Secondly, use your questioning skills to help her score. The following questions will help:

Career

What does a good day at work look like?

How do you rate your performance at work?

How do you feel about your relationships with your colleagues?

How do you feel about work when you walk into the office?

Money

How satisfied are you with your salary?

What would your ideal income be?

How would having more money change your daily life?

How do you feel when you check your bank balance?

Health

What exercise do you do and enjoy?

How would you describe a perfectly healthy 'you'?

What would your ideal daily diet be?

How do you feel in your body?

Friends and family

What do you enjoy doing with your friends?

What would be your ideal way to connect to your family?

What thoughts run through your mind when you think about friends and family?

How much time would you ideally spend with them?

Significant other/love

How are your interests compatible with your partner's?

To what level are your needs being met in your relationship?

How has your relationship grown over the years?

If your relationship was different, how would you love to see it?

Personal growth

What fascinates or excites you?

What skills or knowledge would you most value?

How often do you learn something new?

What does personal growth mean to you?

Fun and recreation

What is your favourite way to relax?

How often does that happen?

Describe your vision of a fun day?

How do you incorporate fun into your life right now?

Physical environment

What would you like to change in your home?

What annoys you about your home?

What works well at home?

Which is your most relaxing room?

Step 3

Once your coachee has scored each spoke, ask her to join up the scores in a dot-to-dot style. The completed wheel might look something like the diagram shown opposite.

If her scores range from low to high, you will end up with a wheel with very jagged edges. Now imagine if this was a bicycle wheel and you were trying to ride it – it would make for a very difficult ride. Alternatively, if each score was very low, you'd end up with a tiny wheel – imagine the effort it would take to get anywhere.

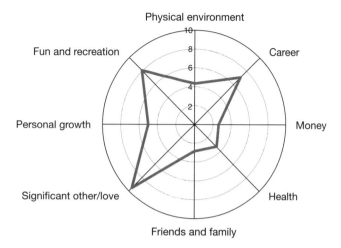

The wheel therefore represents a visual picture of the kind of ride your coachee will be experiencing through life. For an equilibrium to be achieved the wheel has to become smoother and bigger; in short, life will feel more balanced if each spoke reaches a higher number.

Step 4

Given that your coachee can now see the score she has given to each section of her life, this next part is about helping her to evaluate which area of her life she thinks she needs to deal with first.

You could ask:

> **'Which spoke makes sense to you to start with?'**
>
> **'Which topic needs to be dealt with first?'**
>
> **'Which spoke is your priority right now?'**

It is likely that your coachee will notice one spoke, which, if dealt with first, would have an impact on other spokes in her life; remember that a woman's life's topics are always interlinked.

Step 5

Once you have a clear topic, use your goal setting and questioning skills to help your coachee to form a SMART or FEMALE goal for the session. Then you can continue with the TGROW model.

Note: do not assume that the lowest scoring spoke will be the best place to start. A particularly low scoring spoke may represent an area that feels too intimidating or complex to look at initially. You may need to build up a relationship of trust with your coachee first, or she may simply feel too overwhelmed to deal with it at the moment.

Often, improving an area with a medium score first can bring up the lower scoring spokes even though they aren't the primary focus. One of our coachees, Mary, scored her relationship with her 'significant other' at a 3. She explained that they never seemed to have fun together like they used to and if they did go out, they didn't know what to talk about. She didn't want to focus on that area because she was, in her words, 'fed up with trying to make things better'. She felt more enthusiastic about looking at how to improve her happiness in her career which had scored a reasonably healthy 7. Her goal for the session was to find three strategies which would bring her score up to 9.5.

By the end of the session, these were Mary's three strategies:

- To change her belief that she had to be involved in every aspect of her company for it to flourish.

- To commit to delegating mundane administrative tasks.

- To put boundaries in place for when she could be contacted by colleagues.

Mary later explained that those strategies would in fact end up having an impact on her relationship's low score. Future attempts to talk to her partner about their relationship wouldn't be interrupted by work calls, plus she would have more energy for the relationship if she delegated tasks and limited her involvement with every area of her company.

The following example illustrates how this works with a coachee who has no idea where to begin. This was what one of our coachees said at the beginning of her session – she has very kindly given us permission to share her story with you:

> I don't know where to start. At work I'm really not getting on with my line manager. She's trying to micro-manage me and I hate that. My team aren't pulling together either. Every morning someone's bitching about someone else or about their own workload and expecting me to sort it out for them. My home is a mess, stuff everywhere, no one throws anything away and it desperately needs to be redecorated but I never have the time or energy to do it myself or the money to get in a decorator. I'm worried about money because my pay has been frozen because of the cuts. My health isn't that great either. I've got lots of slightly worrying, niggling aches and pains, and I could certainly do with losing a few pounds and getting fitter. I never have time to see my friends and family or have any fun, and I don't feel I'm developing or moving forward in my career either … where do we start?!'

In this case, there are actually twelve potential topics. Here they are in bullet points:

- Line manager
- Atmosphere at work
- Being micro-managed
- Team
- Workload
- Home
- Energy levels/health
- Financial situation
- Friends/family
- Fun
- Fitness level
- Career development

On this occasion, we put them into a wheel, where each spoke represented its own topic:

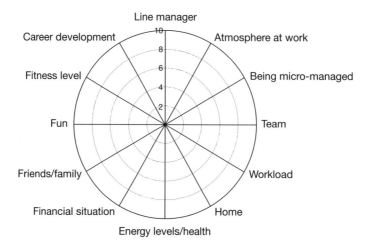

You would then follow steps 1–5 as detailed above.

Here are a few other examples of how this versatile tool can be used.

Example 1

Choosing a career:

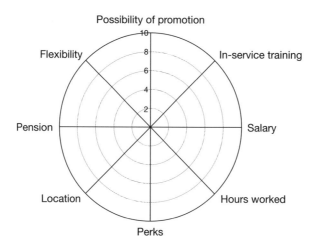

Example 2

As part of our coaching diploma course, we encourage students to work on their own wheel of confidence so they can assess where they are while developing their coaching skills.

A typical wheel for our coaching students would look like this:

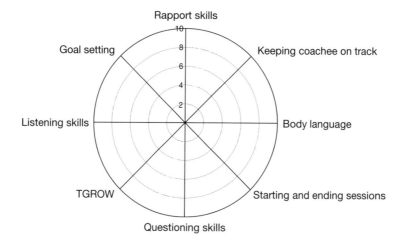

Example 3

Trainee coaches could also do a setting up in business wheel:

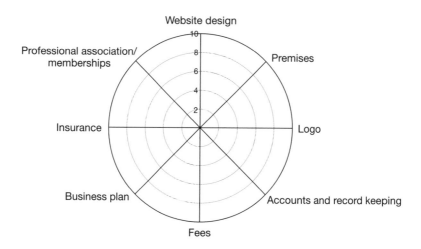

Any one of those spokes could form its own wheel too, for instance, if we take the 'website design' spoke:

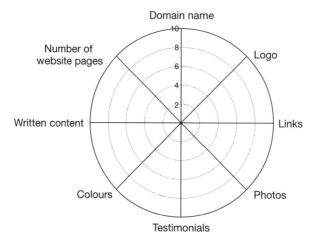

Example 4

We have also seen a wheel of strife – an amusing way to look at what is stressing your coachee:

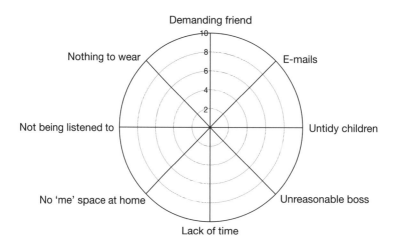

Once the areas have been identified your coachee can see how improving her score on any one of the spokes could make life less stressful.

Example 5

Our coachees have used the wheel very effectively at work too. It is a helpful exercise when a number of people are working in a team but aren't clear who is doing what or even what they are all working towards. Getting each member of the team to draw a wheel and to name the spokes according to the eight top priorities of a given project can pinpoint visually where people have differing ideas about what is happening. It highlights where people may be seeing things very differently to their colleagues, so agreeing on a wheel for the whole team can bring clarity and focus.

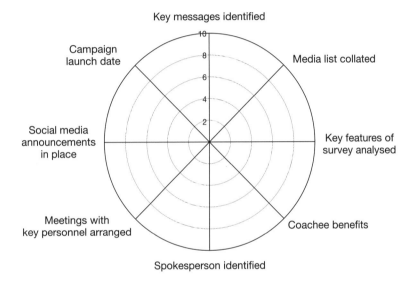

For on-going projects coachees can score and date their wheels, then re-score and re-date to chart and manage progress effectively.

Example 6

The wheel can also be used to compare two or more different options, for example, whether to live in Cambridge or Aldeburgh. In this instance, your coachee would identify what matters to her in choosing where to live. One of our coachees, Sally, used this particular wheel and her areas were:

- House prices
- Distance from friends and family
- Proximity to the sea

- Local schools
- Shops
- Entertainment
- Transport links
- Quality of golf courses

These criteria became the spokes of her wheel and she was able to score each town in a different line stroke to get a visual picture of how near or far each was from her ideal home.

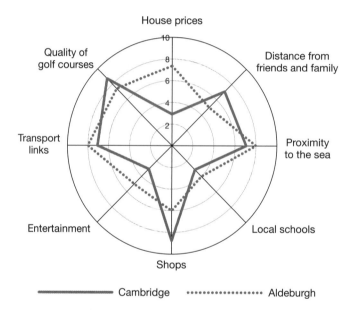

Women and the wheel of life

One of the reasons we find the wheel of life particularly effective for women is because it gives them the time and opportunity to think about and express the emotions attached to each spoke (Key Principle 4). How often does a woman get the chance to reflect on her thoughts and emotions in the company of someone whose only concern is that she finds an answer that suits her? We are not in any way suggesting that our male counterparts don't have this ability; they do, and we've coached men who have worked with this exercise and appreciated, if not welcomed, the space it has given them to map out their thoughts and the associated emotions that go with them. In their book *Brainsex*, Moir and Jessel state that 'man keeps his emotions in their place; and that place is on the right side of the brain, while the power to express his feelings in speech lies over on the other side'. In other words, men keep their emotions and speech in different boxes within their brain. From this, they deduce that it is more difficult for a man to express his emotions than it is for a woman whose 'emotional capacities (are) on both sides of the brain ... and the emotional side is more integrated with the verbal side of the brain' (1998: 48).

Women, it seems, use these two compartments together which explains our need (not just our skill) to express our emotions.

This capacity to talk about her emotions will help the coachee to understand and express what she is feeling about the areas she has chosen for the spokes of her wheel. Moir and Jessel also say of women that 'the bias of her brain leads her to attach much more importance [than a man does] to the personal and interpersonal aspects of life' (1998: 100), so she will highly value the insights she gets from using this very visual tool. Furthermore, 'her relationships are those of interplay, complement and association' (1998: 101), so she will really get to feel how the different aspects of her life or of a project are interconnected. Her coach is often the one person who can do this within a confidential environment, and your female coachee will cherish that time.

11 The Values of a Woman Today

When a coachee comes to you because she feels uncomfortable with a situation or a decision, she may not know why. We've seen this hundreds of times, where a woman isn't 'in flow' with her life, her partner, her work or her family – where something is grating. You may hear phrases such as 'It just doesn't feel right,' 'I can't put my finger on what's wrong' or even 'I have the perfect life but I'm just not enjoying it any more.' Those phrases can be pretty scary to a new or inexperienced coach, and also to a woman who is used to feeling in control. The problem with these statements is that they are not specific in the slightest and give the coach very little clue as to how to start the session. So what can you do?

When a coachee genuinely doesn't seem to know where to start or what the main problem is, you could introduce them to the core values exercise. Some coaches do this exercise as a precursor to coaching but it is also a very valuable stand-alone self development tool.

Core values are particular to each person. They are the values by which they feel they need to live their life in order for them to feel balanced, stable and fulfilled. They include the personal values that mean the most to them and that make up their individuality. We've heard core values described as 'guiding stars' – our navigational aids through life. The trouble is that, often, we are not really conscious of what our core values are. Instead of shining brightly to lead us where we want to be, they are hidden behind a cloud made up of all the daily stresses and demands which stop us from spending time finding out what we most value. It is often the reason many of us work hard to get somewhere but still feel discontented when we reach our goal.

You may hear coachees saying things like:

> **'I worked really hard to get to where I am but now I'm here something's still missing'**

or

> **'I've got everything I ever dreamed of and more but I still feel discontented.'**

The coachee will have a feeling of unease or emptiness, a sense that she should be doing something else, but she can't put her finger on why or what. She will find that she fills her time with things she doesn't really care about or want to do. Not knowing what her most important values are also means she won't be prioritising properly. Many women spend most of their time and energy trying to keep things running smoothly at home and at work, so they simply don't have the space to stop to think about what is really important to them. If they do think about it, they probably just think longingly of having a holiday or getting some peace and quiet – lovely, of course, but not likely to bring a true sense of lasting fulfilment.

Core values define what life means to us. Your coachee's core values could include concepts such as:

truth	making the most of each day	health	honour
trust	self development	peace	support
respect	making a difference	freedom	safety
empathy	learning	reflection	adventure
understanding	kindness	authenticity	core strength
vitality	spirituality	intimacy	vulnerability
security	integrity	achievement	being unique
choice	passion	friendship	individuality
fairness	doing your best	self reliance	legacy
growth	energy	stability	connection

But they may also include more tangible things that are really valuable in someone's life, such as:

the sea
food
blue skies
fresh air
travel

Core values are the silent motivators behind your coachee's decisions and therefore shape the goals she sets. They define who she is and what actions she takes. Not knowing her core values or ignoring them often means getting stressed, feeling confused about decisions, feeling something is missing, not knowing who she is and ultimately questioning the value of her life. Knowing *how* her core values are missing from her life will help her to understand what is holding her back and give her choices in how she wants to behave. If your coachee's goals are aligned with her core values, she will have unstoppable true motivation.

How does the core values exercise work?

You will need to explain to your coachee that the exercise usually takes about an hour to complete. We don't recommend that our coachees do the exercise on their own. Spending time really thinking about what matters to you can be a very emotional experience, particularly if you discover that you've ignored or forgotten what matters most. So having your coach present with you to promote forward thinking about how to incorporate your newly realised values into your life from today onwards will back up this exercise.

In the spirit of being completely non-directional you will, of course, need your coachee's permission to start this exercise. Explain the reasons behind the core values exercise and ask your coachee if she thinks it sounds appealing. If she says yes, go ahead and start. Keep in mind the six key principles throughout this exercise, just as you would during a TGROW coaching session. Ask her to list the ten values she thinks are most important to her, in no particular order. You can give a few examples to illustrate what you mean if you wish, but be very careful that your coachee understands these are just examples and not what you think she ought to have as her own values. Reassure her that it doesn't matter in what order she names her values – the most important may not come out first.

Another tip is to explain that we are not talking about things like world poverty or hunger or ending wars. This exercise is about the personal not the global.

Some coachees find articulating their values very easy while others may need help. You can facilitate by asking questions such as:

> **'What was important to you in childhood?'**
>
> **'What makes you angry/sad/frustrated?'**
>
> **'What behaviour would you defend?'**
>
> **'What's unfair to you?'**
>
> **'What do you admire most about other people?'**
>
> **'When you were happy, what were you doing?'**
>
> **'What did you feel when things were going well?'**
>
> **'What inspires you to take action?'**
>
> **'What drives you crazy?'**
>
> **'When things aren't going well, what do you feel is missing?'**
>
> **'On your 90th birthday what do you want to celebrate about your life?'**
>
> **'On your deathbed what would you have had to have done to stop yourself saying *If only*?'**
>
> **'What does that tell you about your core values?'**

When you have ten values (named in either one word or a short phrase) ask your coachee to come up with four words or phrases to describe each of her values (see the example opposite). This ensures that both coach and coachee understand precisely what the coachee means when using these words.

This is helpful for clarity on both sides. It also gives the coachee the opportunity to talk in more detail about her values, bringing in Key Principle 2 – that women learn best through discussion and have highly developed verbal skills. If she is confused, this time will be enormously valuable.

It is also important to make sure you and your coachee understand her version of a word or the significance of that word in her life.

'Friendship', for instance, will mean one thing to one person and something quite different to another. It may also be interesting to note any descriptive words that come up more than once – when this happens there is often a value 'theme' running through their clarifying words that could help your coachee identify how best to move forward.

Here are some examples of values we've heard from coachees when doing this exercise. The value words are in bold and the four descriptive words/phrases are in italics.

Learning – *interaction, stimulation, interest, being absorbed*

Financial security – *independence, choice, peace of mind, energy*

Partnership – *warmth, sharing, fun, support*

Friendship – *connection, fun, sharing, companionship*

Travel – *broader world view, challenge own beliefs, pleasure, excitement*

Creativity – *sense of achievement, delight, new things, challenge*

Challenge – *excitement, opportunity to use brain, come up with answers, opportunities*

Good health – *energy, opportunity to enjoy life in general, less stress, peace of mind*

Freedom – *choices, independence, making my own decisions, being alive*

Tea shops – *being nurtured, connection to others, stimulation, warmth*

You will notice there are a number of repetitions in the list – that is fine. We learn so much from noticing the words we repeat and discussing the significance of them. When we do the core values exercise, we write down what our coachees say to leave them free to think. We also offer to e-mail the list to them soon after the session.

Once your coachee has listed her values we then 'stress test' them. What we are aiming for is to narrow down ten important values to just three – her most important. If core values are meant to be a navigational aid when making decisions or creating goals, then being able to recall the three most important ones quickly will mean they can be referred to in order to help bring clarity to any situation.

These top three values may come as a complete surprise to the coachee so don't let her guess at the top three! This may explain why her current situation is making her feel so uneasy. After all, if you've been trying all your life to get to what you presumed was important to you, and it turns out to be last on your list, then you won't feel as fulfilled as you thought you would be.

How to stress test your coachee's values

Start with the first value they gave you (i.e. 'learning' in the example above) and ask your coachee to choose between 'learning' and the next one down, which in this case is 'financial security'. Give the value they choose 1 point and the value they discard 0. Then ask them to choose between 'learning' and the next one down 'partnership' and continue scoring 'learning' against each of the following values until you reach the bottom. When you reach the bottom, go back up to the top and choose the second value 'financial security' to test. Ask your coachee which they prefer between 'financial security' and the next one down 'partnership'. Continue in exactly the same way until all the words have been tested against 'financial security'. Go back to 'partnership' and test the remaining values against it. Carry on down the list, testing each value against the ones *below* it in the list (remember you don't need to go backwards up the list).

If your coachee has problems deciding between two values, remind her about the four words or phrases she used to describe what each value gives her. Now simply add up all the 1's that each value earned and you will have a table that looks something like this:

Learning	0	1	1	1	1	1	1	1	1	8
Financial security	1	0	1	1	0	0	0	1	1	5
Partnership	0	1	0	0	1	1	1	1	0	5
Friendship	0	0	1	1	1	0	0	1	0	4
Travel	0	0	1	0	1	1	1	1	1	6
Creativity	0	1	0	0	0	1	1	1	0	4
Challenge	0	1	0	1	0	0	0	0	0	2
Good health	0	1	0	1	0	0	1	0	0	3
Freedom	0	0	0	0	0	0	1	1	0	2
Tea shops	0	0	1	1	0	1	1	1	1	6

Your coachee's top three values have been revealed. In this example, they are 'learning' (which scored 8) and joint second place 'travel' (which scored 6) and 'tea shops' (which scored 6).

Incidentally, if the coachee chooses a family member or friend as one of her values, ask her instead to name the quality she associates with the person rather than the person themselves. When you are asking her to choose between the values, it will be far easier to make the choice between 'friendship' and 'travel' than between her actual best friend and another value.

Core values can often be very helpful to the coachee when they have to make a decision. For instance, if someone asks your coachee to do her a favour and she feels uncomfortable about it, she can now assess how doing that favour would fit into her top values. For example, someone who is asked to take on a rescue pet may feel it could be a good thing to do but if her top value is 'travel', it will be obvious why she is uncomfortable with it.

Ask your coachees to identify the best way for them to remember their core values once they are back in their own hectic lives. Some people write them down, others learn them by heart; your coachee may choose a completely different method. By identifying their top three, it is important to remember that you are not devaluing the other seven – but remembering and running through ten values every time you want to draw on this exercise could be a time consuming process. Every value on the list will be special to them and for major choices (or if they feel they've lost their way) they might like to use all ten in their evaluation process.

Ideally, all of our values and any of the themes which come up in the descriptive words should have a place in our lives, but sometimes it might be necessary to choose to set aside a value for a specific period of time in order to achieve a more urgent goal. For example, someone wanting to save for a deposit on a house could chose to ignore a top value of 'travel' while saving up. The important thing is that values aren't forgotten and are only ever ignored when a conscious choice has been made.

The following are a few examples from coachees in our own practices who have come to their sessions saying:

> **Tracey:** I find it so difficult to say no to people, whether I'm being asked to put in extra hours at work or asked to help friends by babysitting. I've tried all sorts of strategies and while they work for a short time, I always go back to my old habits.
>
> **Amy:** I'm happy at work but I have this niggly feeling that I should be doing something else and I don't know why.
>
> **Anna:** I've always thought of myself as a mother first and now all my children have left home I've lost a sense of who I am.
>
> **Victoria:** Everything should be perfect – I've got a great marriage, a job I love and we've bought the dream house but I keep feeling something is missing.
>
> **Jenny:** I'm finding it really difficult to decide whether to give up my job and start my own company. I've talked to lots of people about it, spent time researching, made lists of pros and cons but I'm still stuck.

How did doing the core values exercise help? Let's look at them in more detail.

Tracey: I find it so difficult to say no to people whether I'm being asked to put in extra hours at work or asked to help friends by babysitting. I've tried all sorts of strategies and while they work for a short time, I always go back to my old habits.

This is about Tracey genuinely trying to change her behaviour but never being able to make the changes last. Doing the core values exercise identified that she had a top value of 'feeling respected'. She translated this into everyday life by acknowledging that she needed to earn respect by being capable of doing everything asked of her. She realised though that she couldn't see the link between 'feeling respected' and 'saying no' which is why she'd always go back to saying yes. Knowing that she needed to feel respected gave Tracey the option of looking for other ways to feel respected. Instead of needing to say yes to everything she realised she could be respected for other talents. In fact she told her coach she was already getting respect, firstly as a valued team leader at work and secondly as the most diplomatic person on the board of school governors. She just hadn't noticed respect coming from these places before because she didn't know what she was looking for. Once she realised this, she started to say no to anything she didn't really want to do, which incidentally also gave her more self respect.

Amy: I'm happy at work but I have this niggly feeling that I should be doing something else and I don't know why.

This example came from Amy, a teacher. She knew she loved working with children and that it was important to her to make a difference in the world. Teaching seemed to be the perfect fit but she found herself repeatedly wondering if this was really the job for her. The core values exercise showed her what was missing. One of her top values was 'feeling valued'. Her teenage pupils didn't often express their appreciation and parents were more focused on their child's progress than on thanking her as the teacher. Knowing what was missing helped Amy to look for other ways of feeling valued at work. She asked her head of year to give her positive feedback when she deserved it. She realised that she could give herself a feeling of being valued by noticing when a pupil was really enjoying a piece of work or had a breakthrough in trying to learn something. Once she found what was missing she relaxed back into her job.

Anna: I've always thought of myself as a mother first and now all my children have left home I've lost a sense of who I am.

Anna became a mother very young in life. It is all she wanted to do, in fact, so when she had her first child she decided to give up work and concentrate on bringing up her child. Ten years later, Anna had three children. Life was hectic, which she loved, each child was popular and there was a constant stream of children in and around the house. Being a mum even extended to mothering her children's friends; often they would spend the night and go to her with problems instead of their own parents. Over time though, her children grew up and naturally spent more time out of the house, until the point when each of them went to university for the first time. With no one at home to mother, and having started her family so young, Anna found herself in her forties and unsure of her role and who she was. Her top three values ended up being 'compassion', 'understanding' and 'respect'. Anna explained that she had intuitively used these three values while bringing up her family and felt disappointed that her children's friends' families often seemed not to encompass those values in their lives. Anna decided to train to become a social worker and use these values in her work. She now has a dual purpose: being a mum to grown-up children and working with families and young children in her district, which ticks all of her boxes.

Victoria: Everything should be perfect – I've got a great marriage, a job I love and we've bought the dream house but I keep feeling something is missing.

Throughout her thirties Victoria built the life she wanted: she married someone she loved, bought a house and worked hard to cultivate the job that suited her perfectly, but reaching the end of her thirties she couldn't shake the feeling something was missing. Victoria used the core values exercise to elicit 'adventure' as her top value. When she looked more closely at her lifestyle, she noticed a distinct lack of adventure and, once identified, was able to put plans into place that meant she could incorporate this during her forties. The fit was perfect for her and she started a list of all the adventurous things she wanted to include in her life.

Jenny: I'm finding it really difficult to decide whether to give up my job and start my own company. I've talked to lots of people about it, spent time researching, made lists of pros and cons but I'm still stuck.

When Jenny arrived at her coaching session she described how comfortable her job was. She loved the people and could do the work in her sleep, but she had always wondered if she could make more money and have a stronger sense of job satisfaction if she worked for herself. The traditional ways of debating her dilemma hadn't worked so coaching was her next option. When she worked through her core values she realised that 'trust' was her top value. Initially, Jenny didn't see how trust could help her with her decision, but using the rest of her session to talk about what it meant to her, part of its meaning was to be able to 'trust her own instincts'. It was important that she was able to trust herself. Jenny realised that if she knew she could trust her own instincts she would have no hesitation in starting her own business. Her mind made up, she began to put her plan together and start her own company.

We are so often asked if core values stay the same throughout our lives. We think that intrinsically they do but that they may be expressed in different words at different times in our lives and priorities might change from decade to decade. For example, a coachee had 'cooking' as a top value in her forties but said that in her twenties she hardly knew how to boil an egg. What matters is what 'cooking' meant to her – creativity, pleasing her senses, entertaining people and doing something well. In her twenties she had loved singing in a band which gave her exactly the same outcomes, except that she was pleasing her ears not her palate!

In our experience, we find that coachees usually like to reflect on the results of their core values exercise before working out how to incorporate them into their everyday lives. Generally this comes in a future coaching session. You might find that it is the topic of the next session or you might even find you could use the wheel of life exercise to ascertain the extent to which their values are already apparent in their lives. Below is an example of what a values wheel might look like.

You would use the wheel exactly how we've shown you, by scoring how integrated each value is, with 0 being at the very centre of the wheel and 10 being at the very edge of the wheel. Once each value has been given a score, you can join the dots up and see how wonky the wheel is!

You might find the following questions very helpful during this process:

> **'How much is freedom honoured in your daily life?'**
>
> **'How much is security given a priority?'**
>
> **'What score would you give creativity right now?'**
>
> **'What happens in your life to honour your sense of fun?'**

As with the previous wheel examples, your coachee may choose one of these areas for her main topic and goal for the session.

So, as you can see, whatever your situation, however old you are, whatever your job or background, core values are personal and important to everyone, both men and women. We spoke to Rebecca Hourston of Move Mountains (www.move-mountains.co.uk). She's also part of the Aspire team at Aspire Companies (www.aspirecompanies.com), which focuses on leadership, development, coaching and events for women. We asked her opinion on whether women and men work differently with their values during a coaching session. She says that values, ethics and beliefs are almost an 'unexpressed thing':

> To really help a coachee move forward in their life I believe it goes back to the coach creating good foundations for work with their coachee. For me, it's always about finding out what my coachee's values are first and then making sure that their overall plans and goals are aligned and tied in with them and their ethics and beliefs. If they're not, you're on a non-starter. The more that any goal is tied in with the coachee's values and personal ethics, the more the coachee will be drawn to it and the better chance they have of feeling emotionally linked to it.

> Our values are what we stand for, what most matters to us in life. As a coach, it's about being alert as to what makes your coachee come alive, what lights them up when you talk to them; it's an intricate overlapped web of values, ethics and beliefs. Several of my female coachees have wanted to be coached on how to achieve promotion, overseas promotion in particular, and one of the first things we explore is how it would fit with the other things in her life (i.e. the broader aspects of her life, including children, if she has them or wants to have them). If

I don't do that, then I know I won't be tapping into that integral part of what matters most to her. If you want to help your coachee to get back in touch with her core values you'll need to understand how to explain the core values exercise. If my coachees say they want X, but upon further coaching realise that gaining X could on some level upset those other things they hold dear, then even the best laid plans in the world aren't going to feel right for them.

I find that it's absolutely essential for a woman's goals to be linked to her values, to what matters most to her. Women think they're drowning when they're going along a path or being propelled along a path where their values aren't being considered, where something jars – it's important to men too but it's the classic head/heart argument that says men will move towards a goal by putting procedural steps in place to get them to that desired end goal, whereas women are more likely to agonise over matching values with goals and the consequences of each of those procedural steps. She'll consider what impact they will have on those involved and how that impact can be mitigated.

To illustrate, Rebecca goes on to compare the path that her male coachees tend to take in relation to their careers and the path her female coachees take:

For men it's more of a career ladder, it's step by step forwards and upwards, it's logical and sequential on the whole; for women it's more of a career tree, that is, the decisions they make involve sideways steps, involve different branches, they generally have more to encompass in their lives, more external factors to consider, her path is more likely to need to be flexible. Often a straightforward sequential ladder won't fit her values; she's more likely to need to make all the connections in her life work and need to consider the knock-on effects and implications. A career tree helps women to normalise what they're going through.

Whatever your coachee is facing, the core values exercise is never wasted. Not only is it an opportunity for your coachee to discover more about herself and how she's made up, but it works beautifully with the key principles, especially Key Principle 4

– women are emotionally literate and so are willing to acknowledge, explore and express emotions. The core values exercise can bring up a lot of emotional issues attached to why your coachee has or hasn't involved key core values in her life before. It can be a steep learning curve. Please note that this doesn't mean a man wouldn't or couldn't be emotional about discovering his core values; it is just that typically, through our research and experience, a woman is more likely to share the emotions behind her values with you.

In short, by exploring her values, you can guarantee that she will find the key and template to help her make many future decisions in everyday circumstances and in major life changes.

12 Beliefs and Their Link With Emotions

Nothing is but thinking makes it so.

Hamlet, II, ii

A person's beliefs, whether they are a man or a woman, will be deeply ingrained and will have a profound effect on their lives. If these beliefs are negative, the discomfort that those beliefs bring will be having a direct influence on how your coachees view the world and live their lives. The discord that comes from our limiting self/life beliefs can have devastating effects on our dreams and ambitions. Beliefs have the ability to either underpin and strengthen plans and actions, or they can trip us up, making us feel uneasy, uncertain and less committed to change.

The unique views we have of ourselves and the world dictate how we interact with others, what jobs we do, how we live on a daily basis, what we eat and where we set up home – they affect everything we do.

Our beliefs are built up over a lifetime – everything from an individual's childhood, parental influences, schooling and work, to their marriages, divorces, successes and failures will form their view of the world. This is a very personal sense of how they see themselves, what they feel capable of and what they deem to be true about the world. Because our belief systems are established in early childhood, when we are too young to put negative remarks and comments into context, our beliefs about ourselves and the world can be unhelpfully destructive.

We've had many coachees who were told as children, for instance, 'you could do better'. The adult saying this, whether a parent or teacher, is most likely to have been a caring adult trying to do their best for the child. But the child only hears 'I'm not good enough', believes it is the truth and carries on through life only noticing those events which confirm this negative view. A child who is told she's no good at maths may grow up noticing every time she makes a numerical mistake and might never notice the times she gets it right. By the same token, a girl who is told she's clumsy will remember the one time she dropped a cup while washing up but not all the times she didn't drop anything. Beliefs tend to become absolute and global: 'I'm clumsy' and never 'I sometimes bump into my desk'. You will remember from the chapter on the unconscious that our minds are literal – they store information easily and readily, especially negative information. They store it as *our* truth; therefore, we always get the proof of our beliefs because we only see what we already believe to be true.

It is astonishing how easy it is to pile up evidence for a negative belief. We act out what we believe about ourselves and consequently get back the results we think we deserve. We heard a story about a woman who went to a party believing she was a boring person who no one would want to talk to. As a shy child she had been embarrassed by adults remarking that she hadn't got much to say for herself, so she grew up feeling that she wasn't capable of being interesting. At the party, her expectations of being ignored became a reality because she hardly spoke to anyone all evening – yet more proof to shore up her negative self belief of 'I'm boring and no one wants to talk to me'. The interesting thing was that in the days after the party, several people said they hadn't spoken to her because her body language said 'leave me alone' or because they thought she was being antisocial by not making an effort. If she had gone to the party believing that people would react warmly to her, then her body language would have been different, her facial expressions and energy would have been welcoming and she would have been approachable. It was the belief itself which stopped her from socialising, nothing more.

There is a popular saying that 'we create our own universe'. Certainly what we believe about ourselves and the world can shape our lives in the most fundamental way, and changing those beliefs can transform how we live. Coach Anthony Robbins says, 'Before something happens in the world, it must happen in your mind' (2001: 85).

Yet in the normal day-to-day running of things, our beliefs go largely undetected. We don't stop every five minutes when we make a decision and consider what our beliefs around this issue are, we just react. For women and men, our beliefs are so deep that we are largely unaware of them. They are definitely there, although we often don't recognise their very limiting influence on our actions as they silently underpin our decisions and our life plans.

A simple ABC model explains how important our beliefs are in governing what we do and how we feel (see Neenan and Dryden, 2002: 48):

A = activating event (e.g. you imagine asking questions and making comments at a meeting, instead of keeping silent or saying very little, which is your usual pattern of behaviour)

B = beliefs or thoughts (e.g. I'll say the wrong thing or get my facts confused and look like an idiot in the eyes of others)

C = emotional and behavioural consequences (e.g. intense anxiety)

People assume that A causes C but in fact it is what is happening at B which causes C. What happens at B, the beliefs someone has, can result in very different outcomes, for instance:

A = activating event (e.g. the end of a relationship)

B = beliefs or thoughts (e.g. without her I'm worthless)

C = emotional and behavioural consequences (e.g. depression and withdrawal from social activity)

A = activating event (e.g. the end of a relationship)

B = beliefs or thoughts (e.g. thank goodness that's over)

C = emotional and behavioural consequences (e.g. I'm free! I'll go out and celebrate)

One of the most powerful results of being coached can be your coachee's realisation that a belief is not a fact, as they once thought it was. Many of the things we believe to be solid, indisputable truths about ourselves are just thoughts that somehow we perceive to be true. If this is the case, then we can choose to change them. As Anthony Robbins observes, all personal breakthroughs must start with a change in beliefs.

As a coach you should be aware that for some people this fact is quite frightening. All of a sudden they realise that what they've believed about how hopeless they are or how they can't change anything isn't actually an unalterable truth written in stone.

That means either they need to think about what they do want instead and work out how to get it, or make a conscious choice to do nothing and stay stuck. In other words, it brings with it enormous personal responsibility.

Often our beliefs are linked to the stereotypes we have about men and women. Both genders are affected by conventional belief systems but the ideas themselves are frequently linked to what we expect of ourselves as women or men. A man, for instance, may measure himself against an ideal of masculinity – to be strong, a provider, a hero, the highest achiever at work; whereas a woman may measure herself against the superwoman image – someone who nurtures her family, makes things run smoothly for everyone else, is sexy and attractive at all times, looks forever young and manages a high flying position at work. So although both genders may say 'I'm not good enough', they may mean very different things.

It is important that you know your coachee's definition of her beliefs, as it will help you to create that unique relationship with her (Key Principle 1). It is about noticing and honouring her beliefs as part of the coaching process – that is why she is coming to you.

The following beliefs are just some that we've heard from our female coachees:

> **'I'm too young to …'**
>
> **'I'm too old to …'**
>
> **'I'm incompetent.'**
>
> **'You only get anywhere by working until you are exhausted.'**
>
> **'Life's not meant to be easy.'**
>
> **'Only men get the top jobs.'**

You can see how these negative beliefs have imprisoned some of the women we've coached. If you genuinely believe that life is not meant to be easy, you will ignore opportunities that come your way and see problems in everything. Your attention will be drawn towards what has gone wrong, not what went right. Someone who thinks we are meant to work until we are exhausted won't see that it is possible to earn a living from something you enjoy doing. With this self limiting belief, work is something to be endured and opportunities to work with passion and joy aren't likely to be considered. It will be useless anyone telling you that life can be easy and run smoothly because you will have spent a lifetime gathering information to prove the negative belief you've chosen to live by is, in fact, the truth. The sad part is that there will have been just as many or more times when everything went well for that person or they got results from minimum effort. But because their antennae were tuned in to their 'life isn't easy' mantra, they simply won't have noticed them.

So how do you recognise if your female coachee is being held back by her belief system?

You might hear statements such as 'I'm not clever enough to do that,' 'I *always* make the wrong decision,' 'I'm incapable of meeting deadlines' and 'I'm *never* organised.' Before you pounce in triumph to identify your coachee's negative belief for them, remember Key Principle 6 – that women are more self critical than men. Women have a tendency to put down themselves and their achievements, so this doesn't automatically indicate a serious self belief issue. There are all sorts of reasons why women do this, ranging from consciously helping those around them to feel better about themselves or not wanting to appear over confident and bullish – not helpful, we grant you, but very common nevertheless. So we are asking you to notice, to flag this up to your coachee and to reflect back to them what you hear and to work with their responses. Take a soft approach when working on a coachee's beliefs and you will find that your gently probing questions will promote discussion, while your straightforward approach to asking direct questions (with care) will invite your coachee to consider what is holding her back, whether her beliefs serve her well and if they are still current and applicable in her life. And if they aren't, what can replace them.

Let's take an example of two fictional women who we will call Sarah and Rachel.

Sarah can always be found cheerful and smiling, she never says a negative thing about anyone or any situation, everyone gravitates towards her and she has lots of friends. She's always on time, she's good at her job and has worked her way up through the company steadily. Her colleagues rely on her and know she'll be there when they need her.

Rachel on the other hand can always be relied upon to inject a little reality into everyone's day. She calls herself a 'realist', she never seems happy, she follows every sentence with 'yes but' and her colleagues and friends don't ask her out after work. She's stayed in the same position at work for over five years, is often late and misses deadlines.

What could Sarah's beliefs be?

That working hard rewards you.

That people like her.

That everyone is friendly.

That it is important to be on time.

That it is important to be reliable.

That life is fun.

What do you think Rachel's belief might be?

That working is a chore.

That she is not good at deadlines.

That she is not a 'people person'.

That she is not good at her job.

That everyone else gets promoted above her.

Now imagine that Rachel confides in Sarah and asks her to help her get more organised at work – how might she go about this? She might help her set timetables for her work, she might encourage her to create a tick-list so she doesn't forget things, she might even encourage her to be more positive at work and let her know the 'yes but's' have been noticed and perceived as negative. If Rachel is keen to improve she might change for a short while, but if her beliefs about herself and her work remain unchanged, she is bound to remain unchanged and her old behaviour patterns will re-emerge.

Now imagine that Rachel confided in a coach and asked for help to get more organised:

> *Topic: To be more organised at work*
>
> *Goal: To have two things to do differently to increase her productivity. She currently rates her productivity at a 4 out of 10*
>
> COACH (Q1):   OK Rachel, so you're currently at a 4 out of 10. What would make you feel confident you're at a 5 out of 10?

COACHEE: *... (coachee thinks for a bit)* Good question. I suppose if I was marking someone else at a 5 out of 10, they'd be a 5 and not a 4 if they were mostly on time. I know my time keeping isn't good, it's never been good, I'm just not someone who's organised enough to be on time.

COACH (Q2): What if you were someone who was organised enough to be on time?

COACHEE: Well, that would be great but I just think some people are organised and others aren't. I don't really think I'll ever be organised enough to be on time.

COACH (Q3): So you don't think you can become someone who can be on time?

COACHEE: *(laughs)* No, I really don't!

COACH (Q4): So, given that you don't think you can change to become someone who runs on time, but that someone else would be a 5 and not a 4 in your opinion, because that's exactly what they do, how do we reconcile that difference?

COACHEE: I'm not sure I can. I mean, if I don't believe it can happen, I suppose it won't happen.

COACH (Q5): Is that OK with you?

COACHEE: Well, no, not really. I'd really like to be more organised and one of the things I'd love most is to be able to hand a piece of work in on time and not stress that it's going to be late again, or not worry about my boss's reaction or my next appraisal – it's always brought up and I just have to apologise each year, and each year I get told I need to be more in control of my productivity and I never am.

COACH (Q6): So what needs to change?

COACHEE: Well, if I believed I could change that would probably help. In actual fact, I don't think it's right to be late for things, it's such a poor excuse, it doesn't sit well with me. I really admire people who never have to say that.

COACH (Q7): So, if you believed you could change, what would that feel like?

COACHEE:	A relief I think! It would give me hope and a bit of positivity instead of just knowing that today, again, I'll probably be late or miss another deadline. In fact, sometimes I don't even try any more. I think I'd try harder if I thought I could do it, if I had a different belief.
COACH (Q8):	So how do you go about actually changing that belief?
COACHEE:	I'd look for things in my life when I am on time. I'm sure there must be things I do on time but probably don't notice them. If I noticed when I was on time, that would give me a sense of pride and not failure. Yes, that's what I'll do. The first thing I'll do is notice when I'm on time and the second thing I'll do is have deadlines of my own, say 24 hours before the actual deadline, to work to. That way, I'll try harder to stick to them – you never know I might be early!
COACH (Q9):	Imagine visualising yourself running to time, even being early. Can you describe what you see?
COACHEE:	Err, well I'm smiling, I feel really calm actually – that surprises me, I don't usually feel that calm. I'm walking to my boss's office with confidence, I've emailed my copy to her but I'm going to tell her in person that it's in her in-box. I feel confident and I'm walking with more authority too, other people are smiling at me in the corridor – it feels good!

Now the above is just a snippet of a much longer session, but you can see how the coach digs and probes until the coachee identifies what will make a real difference to the way she works. Also notice that the coach only used the word 'belief' once the coachee had identified that she didn't believe she could change – this is perfect and stops the coach from being directive. What you might also notice is that the coachee doesn't believe that being late is right ethically. What we mean by ethics is someone's personal code of conduct and behaviour that they aspire to live by. Never being on time doesn't sit well with her; somewhere in her psyche she doesn't believe it is correct or right to be late, so there is incongruence between what she believes is ethically correct and the behaviour she displays.

Let's look at the coach's questions in detail to see how Rachel can understand how to change.

In Q1 the coach used the scale of 1–10 that you are now familiar with to judge where she was and her question was solution focused and positive, asking how to nudge her score up to a 5.

Q2 reflected the coachee's own thoughts back to her about being someone who was organised and asked what it might be like to be that person – again, it is positive and forward thinking.

Q3 again echoed the coachee's own words – that she didn't think she could become someone who could be on time. The clarification was phrased as a question.

In Q4 the coach doesn't force the issue or try to assure the coachee that they could change. Friends do this and we don't believe them when they do, nice as it is to hear. In this way the coach acknowledges that this is the coachee's true thought process and simply asks how she would move forward to get to her goal *with* that thought process.

Q5 is such a simple one: 'Is that OK with you?' But it is not a question we get asked every day – it is refreshing and just checks that the coach understands the coachee but also gives the coachee a chance to ask herself if it is OK with her. It is an important question.

Q6 is challenging. It is assuming that something needs to change; the assumption is fine given the coachee's previous statement and is forward thinking and solution oriented.

Q7 is hypothetical. Hypothetical questions give coachees the opportunity to dare to think differently without the need to change reality. They are safe – nothing needs to change – but the coach assumes the possibility for change without pinning the coachee down to her answers. This is where the coachee gets a chance to think with all of the solution making part of her mind, without the pressure that she or others around her normally put on her. It is perfect.

Q8 is the first time the coach has mentioned the word 'belief'. Wading into a coaching session by questioning a coachee's belief systems will get you nowhere. This way, the coachee has brought it up and so it is fine for the coach to run with it, and it works. It brings two actions that could change the coachee's situation.

Q9 taps directly into a woman's most natural method of communication – Key Principle 5 about women's ability to visualise very effectively. The coach is asking the coachee to do this as part of a technique to help bring the image of the coachee being on time to life.

The coaching template

If a coachee is deeply self aware and realises exactly how much her beliefs are affecting her life you could introduce them to a coaching template.

There are four sections to this template. Each section starts with a statement and your coachee completes the statements with what they believe to be true at this moment in time. Here is one from a coachee of ours already filled in:

I believe that life is not:	Therefore I believe life is:
1. Free flowing	Problematic
2. Predictable	Unexpected
3. Easy	Hard work

I believe that I am not:	Therefore I believe I am:
1. Creative	Frustrated
2. Intellectual	Stupid
3. Sophisticated	Naive

The answers were prompted by the coach asking questions to probe clear responses. This example feels rather negative, but it is exactly what the coachee came with so you might experience something similar.

The second part of the exercise gives the coachee the opportunity to reframe her beliefs or find new beliefs that excite and inspire her.

I believe that life is:	Therefore I believe life is:
1. Free flowing	Full of choice
2. Predictable	Exciting
3. Easy	There to enjoy

I believe that I am:	Therefore I believe I am:
1. Creative	An artist
2. Intellectual	Quite clever
3. Sophisticated	Aware

No one expects beliefs to magically change overnight but they can be modified through consistent and conscious effort. Repetition is the key; rather like repeating exercises to build up muscles at the gym, this is like taking your belief muscle to the gym, doing the reps and not making excuses! Ask your coachee how she would like to work with her new beliefs. Some coachees choose to actively seek out evidence for beliefs which would serve them better; others stick up paper reminders where they will see them every day to remind them to repeat their new beliefs to themselves. One woman chose to document evidence of her new beliefs every day in a notebook she bought just for this purpose.

You can ask your coachee to score on a scale of 1–10 how committed she is to her new chosen belief. If the answer is anything less than a 10 then it would be helpful to ask questions like:

> **'What could take your commitment level up a point?'**
>
> **'What support do you need to help you to be more committed?'**
>
> **'What changes might you notice when you change your belief?'**

One thing is for sure, this is a sensitive area for everyone. We define ourselves by what we believe to be true about ourselves and the world. A coaching session is a safe space to work out what we want to believe and to understand how to start the work of replacing limiting, negative beliefs with ones which make our lives happier.

What if you find yourself coaching someone who seems determined to stick to her limiting beliefs? What if she doesn't appear to want options for change? What if she seems so stuck in her story that no amount of clever questioning or forward projecting exercises are moving her on? Very occasionally we have found that a coachee has used coaching to confirm that they are indeed stuck to give them some kind of assurance that 'yes, their life is terrible'. If a coachee sees their coach as the 'expert' (although if you've been clear from the outset this is unlikely), they might be tempted to lay all their troubles out on the table with very clear and rehearsed reasons why they can't shift, why they are stuck or why they've tried everything and nothing has worked. If this happens to you remember that coaching works because coachees want to move forwards. They acknowledge that if their situation is to change, they have to change; they have to take responsibility for making decisions, sometimes difficult ones. If your coachee hasn't come to that reality as yet, she won't move forwards. If your coachee seems particularly stuck on a story from her past, it may be that counselling would be of more benefit to her, so gently suggest that this might be more appropriate at this stage rather than trying to coach her when she feels unable to make progress.

Not everyone can move forwards. This is the time when all of your ethics and responsibility kick in. We all have moments of clarity, when we decide very clearly and firmly that it is time for things to change. But a coach can't bring that moment on, only your coachee can. Trust in your skills as a professional coach to be there for your coachee in your entirety; that also means knowing when to bring the coaching process to a close.

13 Stress, Decisions and Making Her Own Mind Up

Millions of women are making millions of decisions all around the world, in every single time zone, right at this very minute. Some decisions are instinctive and we make them without question, while others need more thought and care. Mothers are making decisions about everything from what their children should eat, to what time they should go to bed and who they mix with. Even when they are in relationships and have someone close to discuss those issues with, women are often still the ones making those key decisions. Many women hold the family purse strings and decide what budgets to work within and how far to stretch the family finances, which in turn affects other decisions such as where they go on holiday, if they extend the mortgage or not, whether to change jobs or go for a promotion. At work, many decisions your female coachees make affect her staff, her coachees, her bosses and her colleagues. Making decisions is second nature.

Occasionally though, the responsibility of those decisions and the influence they have on other people sometimes hits us right between the eyes causing us to feel stress. We spoke to Dr Lillian Nejad, co-author of *Treating Stress and Anxiety* (2008), on decision making:

> The major decision and/or the inability to make the decision triggers the stress response (also called the fight or flight response) because it is perceived as a threat, either internal or external (Cannon, 1932). An external threat can have something to do with the effects of making or not making a decision (like financial loss); whereas, an internal threat may relate to their sense of self or sense of control and competency. These threats, either real or imagined, trigger the physical responses in the body: the sympathetic nervous system is activated and hormones are released to prepare our bodies to either fight the problem or run away from the problem. Unhelpful thoughts exacerbate the process by undermining our sense of safety and confidence:

'I can't cope!', I'm a failure!', 'I'm going crazy!', which in turn increases fear and anxiety and leads to more intense physiological responses.

The fight or flight response has been the prevailing model that describes how humans respond to stress; however, a new model has emerged that may further explain women's unique response to stress called the 'tend and befriend response'. This theory suggests that women's responses to stress have evolved differently to men's responses due to their historical role as primary caretaker which necessitates that they protect both themselves and their offspring. Physiologically, both men and women experience the hormonal release associated with the flight or flight response; however, women may also experience a response associated with the attachment/care giving system involving oestrogen and oxytocin that makes responding through aggression or fleeing less likely, and nurturing and seeking social support more likely. Therefore, women are more likely to 'tend' and 'befriend' rather than 'fight' or 'flee' in response to stress. Tending refers to nurturing activities that increase safety and reduce distress and 'befriending' refers to seeking social support (Taylor et al., 2000). Although the flight or flight response serves a useful and protective function by helping us to physically respond to danger; threats in our society are usually not the kind you can beat to a pulp or escape and avoid forever. So it is good news that women may have other biologically based systems in place to assist us to cope in different, and likely, in more adaptive ways. This may account for how women are able to cope with a variety of stressors for long periods of time and it may even explain why women, on average, live longer than men.

The above theory is further supported by the differences in ways that men and women respond to and cope with stress. Men are more likely to withdraw, use substances to relieve stress, and react with anger and irritability; whereas, women are much more likely to seek social support, particularly from other females. Interestingly, although men do not seek support as much as women, they report benefiting from it just as much, highlighting the importance of social support in reducing the physiological responses to stress (Kirschbaum et al., 1995).

Women are famed for taking everyone else into consideration when they make decisions, so when we have people who depend on us, the importance of the decisions we make increases and so does the pressure. This is often the point your coachees will seek coaching for some internal direction or clarification. Here are a few examples of decisions some of our coachees have come to us with recently:

Clare had an immediate life changing decision to make. She had been offered a promotion which meant an almost immediate relocation to New York and had only days to make it.

Jane had lived in the same town with the same partner for years. She felt trapped and realised she needed to make a decision whether to stay or go.

Jo was a gifted young musician hampered by lack of self confidence. She wanted to find out if her musical career worth taking the risk for and facing her confidence issues.

Maria had set up several successful businesses but never felt she was doing well enough. Should she continue building her company hoping it would give her the validation she needed or quit her lifestyle and travel, hoping she would find what she was missing elsewhere?

All of these women used coaching to talk confidentially, to discuss options and to visualise possible outcomes. Be prepared. Her decisions can be laden with guilt, self doubt and anxiety one minute, and laced with opportunity, excitement and intrigue the next – that balance needs the care and attention that only an expert coach can provide. The session will provide her with the opportunity to talk out loud, thereby stimulating her verbal skills, her multilayered thinking and the quick dexterity of her mind.

If you find yourself sitting in front of a woman with a particularly difficult or stressful decision to make, it could be helpful to find out exactly how that stress is currently affecting her. But how will you know exactly how difficult this decision is for your coachee? How will your coachee know? How does she measure the impact that decision may have on the rest of her life? You've read about the 1–10 scale and about clarifying the meanings of words and making sure that you understand the sense the coachee attaches to a word. It also goes without saying how imperative it is to establish the correct goal for the session and to ensure that it is both SMART and

FEMALE, but we've devised another measuring tool that may be appropriate for your coachees – the stress decision path.

The stress decision path

The stress decision path is visual so it will plug straight in to one of your female coachee's most natural communication styles (Key Principle 5), it is linked to her emotions (Key Principle 4) and it promotes discussion (Key Principle 2). As always, you must get the coachee's permission before you go wading in with this tool, which may or may not be helpful. Not everyone will identify with this technique, not even you, but for those who do it can be a great visual stimulant to form the grounding for your coaching session – a place to start, if you will.

We've often found the stress decision path to be a useful tool to depict where a coachee feels they are and even to work out where they would like to be by the end of the session. In our experience, there are definite steps between being able to make decisions easily and feeling so overwhelmed that you become inactive and confused. We've detailed those steps here.

After you check that your coachee feels comfortable using this tool, ask them which step they find themselves at right now. You will get an understanding of what your coachee is facing and your questions can reflect that. You might also ask which step they would like to be at by the end of the session, which means you are both aiming for the same place. Use this rather like a more detailed 1–10 tool.

Step 1 – Able and productive
We're making hundreds of decisions easily and we're thinking nothing of it – we're in control.

Step 2 – Consciously aware
For some reason, the enormity of a decision is brought to our attention and we realise that our decision is a key influencer.

Step 3 – Stress tested
Knowing Step 2 is making us feel more stressed and we feel quite pressured.

Step 4 – Confusion mode

Because of that pressure we might find it hard to think clearly about smaller decisions.

Step 5 – Procrastination mode

The difficulty in our lack of being able to make even small decisions can lead to procrastination.

Step 6 – Self sabotage

Negative self talk comes into its own here, sabotaging our normal, rational behaviour even further. At this point, we look at how we used to make decisions and worry that the 'old' version of us is gone for good. Coachees often report making small mistakes at this time – missing appointments, losing paperwork, being late, forgetting things or picking unreasonable arguments are all common.

Let's take a look at each of the steps in a bit more detail.

Step 1 – Able and productive

Now we've never known a woman who didn't want to be able and productive! To be in this state of mind, a woman often has to feel in complete control (at least of her own decisions and life), so you may be thinking, 'That's the easy bit then, I wouldn't get a coaching coachee who already feels in control, would I?' 'Why not?' would be our answer.

Do remember Key Principles 2, 3 and 4 here: Key Principle 2 is that women learn best through discussion and have highly developed verbal skills; Key Principle 3 is that women have the ability to fix several problems at the same time, even when they are only talking to you about one issue; and Key Principle 4 is that women are emotionally literate and so are willing to acknowledge, explore and express their emotions. Therefore, just because we are in control and feel OK, happy even, it doesn't mean that we don't appreciate an hour or two to be able to focus without interruption. This is one of the states in which a woman makes her best decisions – when she is able to think through her options without prejudice and use her coach as a sounding board. By discussing the if's and but's of her options, she is more likely to work out which decision is right for her.

Key Principle 2 plays a major role here so give her time and space to talk. This is how your coachee learns the most about herself and her decision, and because she is in 'able and productive' mode, she will be able to act on it confidently. This is about having some space: when a coaching session is in flow it is almost like you've stepped out of your world and you are able to decide how fast or slow you want it to begin again once you step back into it. Your coachees may also decide the order in which they need to do things and where their priorities need to be placed. Even for women who feel totally in control, the luxury of being able to 'see ahead' a little and work out what consequences a certain decision might have, and how she would react to them, can be of enormous value and leave her finishing the session with a sense of conviction.

Step 2 – Consciously aware

At this stage your coachee isn't in meltdown, she is simply aware of the value of her decisions. Often a woman will start a session with phrases such as, 'I have to make the right decision,' 'I don't want to make a mistake' or 'I need to make this go as smoothly as possible.' At this point, it is absolutely possible that, with the right coach and the right approach, the coachee can graduate back up to Step 1, feeling in complete control and able to be productive – this isn't necessarily a downward spiral.

Use scenarios such as:

> **'Imagine you've made absolutely the right decision, what would that feel like?'**
>
> **'Let's say you are a year ahead and you are telling me how smoothly the decision went, what would have been the first thing you did?'**
>
> **'What does the "right decision" look like to you right now?'**
>
> **'Imagine you've made a decision you are happy with and it's working really well, what would you be saying to people?'**

As a coach, what you are doing here is focusing on the positive; you are presuming that everything will run smoothly and that your coachee will make the right choice. This kind of positive re-enforcement is essential. Your coachee needs to know that you have absolute trust in her to be able to do this brilliantly.

The wrong scenarios to use would be:

> **'What mistakes could you make here?'**
>
> **'What could go wrong?'**
>
> **'What's at stake here?'**

By focusing on the negative you could freeze any chance she has of making a good, confident decision. She will assume that if you are talking in the negative, you have doubts over whether she can pull off her plans. She will get a feeling that's what you are inferring. Moir and Jessel explain this sense by referring to a part of the brain (the corpus callosum, which has a larger number of connections in women) which allows a woman to tune into a 'superior switchgear'. They explain that 'women are in general better at recognising emotional nuances in voice, gesture, and facial expression, a whole range of sensory information. They can deduce more from such information because they have a greater capacity than men to integrate and cross-relate verbal and visual information' (1998: 48).

This means that women will see straight through any 'fake' confidence you have in them as a coachee. Remember Key Principle 6 too, that women are naturally self critical – don't make this worse with a negative line of questioning or inference. As we've said above, while your mouth could be saying all the right things, your eyes, facial expressions and body posture could be saying 'Nope! No chance!' Part of your job as a coach is to be genuine and truly believe that your coachee can and should achieve. When you do well, your eyes, body language and facial expressions will all be saying *'You can do this!'* and guess what – your coachee will do it.

By focusing on the positive and presuming that your coachee will make the right decision, you are also making an impact on her unconscious mind. To concentrate her thoughts on good, clever outcomes, you are gearing her up to make decisions that will turn out that way.

Step 3 – Stress tested

In our experience, women start to feel stressed when they sense they are losing control. We've already discussed how important control is to most women. Not being in control is one reason why your coachee might feel harassed but is certainly not the only reason, so never presume anything. Your opening gambit should be one of information gathering, with questions such as:

> **'Tell me more about life right now ...'**
>
> **'What particular aspect of this situation is causing you the most stress?'**
>
> **'If this situation could be broken down into, say, three main areas, what would they be?'**

The last question is really helpful to some women. Whether you choose the option of three, four or five areas, it doesn't really matter (although the lower the better to help keep things in perspective), but essentially you are trying to help your coachee break up her seemingly overwhelming problem into smaller bite-sized chunks.

You might even ask:

> **'If this problem could be broken down into smaller chunks, how many chunks would there be?'**

That way you are giving her total control over breaking her issue down and mirroring back to her that she is in control of this decision. What you are asking for here is information. You are helping her to identify if there is one area of her situation that feels more stressful to her than the others – it may be that this could be her starting point. For some, the area that is causing the most discomfort may also be the last place to start, depending on the coachee's preferences. Remember that your coachee is in control of the session and she should always tell you where her priority lies.

Step 4 – Confusion mode

If your coachee is telling you that she is finding it hard to make small decisions, she may be talking about her confidence levels in the same breath. These two are linked so closely, as Dr Lillian Nejad observed when we spoke to her:

Because women's roles have broadened over the last 50 years, so have their stressors. Women have adapted to this by learning to multi-task, by utilising their executive functions – namely their planning and organisational skills, and by striving for perfection in all areas of their lives including work, social life, raising children, and maintaining a household. And it works. Until it doesn't.

Women's strengths can eventually turn out to be their downfall as the cumulative effect of stress and overcommitment of time and energy – both mental and physical – take their toll, and that can leave them feeling either panicked or, alternatively, paralysed. Complex decisions require higher order thinking and depend upon what is termed the 'executive functions' in the prefrontal cortex of the brain. Higher order reasoning skills include focused attention, planning or organisational skills, and the ability to anticipate outcomes of decisions. Under stress, these skills do not function properly, negatively affecting our concentration and judgement and making us more vulnerable to decision making problems.

This is not about diagnosing the coachee's problems. Remember here Key Principle 4 – women are emotionally literate and so are willing to acknowledge, explore and express their emotions. If your coachee arrives in confusion mode, you will be able to tell immediately: she could be unclear as to even how to start the session or where to begin in telling you what is going on. It might be a complicated situation with many considerations, conversations and opinions to consider. The stress decision path could be an extremely valuable tool for someone who arrives in this state, as you are giving them a tool to help them figure out where to start.

Step 5 – Procrastination mode

If your coachee is in this phase they are putting off decisions. They've decided that no action is the best action. Lillian Nejad says:

> Although women may have additional physiological mechanisms in play to assist them to cope with stress in a variety of ways, they still experience the unpleasantness of the fight or flight response:

shaking, sweating, feeling nauseous, stomach ache, dizziness, etc. These symptoms are not only uncomfortable, but they can be very scary and quite embarrassing. So now, both the original problem and the stress response are threats, and the natural response is to avoid both at all costs. Ironically, avoidance feeds fear rather than diminishes it. The decision now appears much more ominous and daunting, and avoiding one decision has now generalised to avoiding other decisions, even ones that used to be effortless and uncomplicated. It's no surprise that this pattern of unhelpful thoughts, self-defeating behaviours and unpleasant feelings can have a drastic effect on one's identity, and if prolonged, on one's physical and mental health.

If you agree with Edward Young's assertion that 'procrastination is the thief of time', then we would ask you to suspend that belief for the duration of your coaching sessions. The word procrastination often has negative associations and it wouldn't be uncommon for our coachees to have to move past it to get going again. This is not always the best move though. Think about it: procrastination can give our brains time to catch up with reality. Procrastination can give us the well earned rest we need from a decision, so when we come back to it, we can make sense of it in a brand new light. Procrastination can be good, so ask your coachee what it is giving them. We would be likely to ask:

> **'What is procrastination giving you at the moment?'**
>
> **'If you knew you were going to make a decision at some point, when do you think would be the right time?'**
>
> **'If there were two advantages to procrastinating right now, what would they be?'**
>
> **'At what point would procrastination begin to be negative for you?'**

All of these questions (you will notice they are open) will give rise to answers, explanations and thoughts, not simply yes or no responses, and you will also observe that they are entirely judgement free.

Don't forget that procrastination sometimes lets us off the hook too. While we've been busy putting things off or mulling over our choices, unable to make any decisions, let alone the right one, situations change. Other people move on and sometimes render our decisions obsolete – someone else made a decision which meant we didn't have to. For some coachees this will prove to be a positive outcome; for others, they will be feeling out of control and as though someone else is driving their life forward. For those coachees, they will be kicking themselves for not taking an opportunity or for not having the conviction to make their own decision. For them, procrastination won't feel comfortable and they will be helped by you asking questions to aid their recovery, repair any damage already done and put a positive plan in place.

Step 6 – Self sabotage

Healthy self talk (by which we mean the positive, upbeat chatter that goes on inside your mind) is a vital ingredient in making good decisions. When self talk gets negative, we are only beating ourselves up – this is traditionally called self sabotage. When our inner thoughts are negative, we focus only on the negative and expect more of the same. It is not helpful, but it is common. Quite often we are not even aware of how negative our self talk is until it is reflected back to us, and a coach is the perfect person to do just that. Lillian Nejad observes:

> Self monitoring thoughts is a useful way to increase awareness of negative self talk, e.g. 'I can't cope', 'You idiot', or 'Everyone is judging me'. Often a pattern of negative self talk emerges and is linked not only to the specific problem but to other areas of the person's life – these patterns are sometimes called cognitive distortions. Common cognitive distortions associated with anxiety are perfectionistic thinking ('If it's not perfect, then it's not good enough), anticipating disaster ('Everything is going to go wrong, I just know it'), worrying about what other people think ('What if she thinks I'm incompetent') and overgeneralising ('Nothing ever goes my way'). These unhelpful and unrealistic thought patterns usually reflect a more ingrained belief system that a person may not be aware of and only comes to light under stress or during a crisis. These core beliefs about themselves, others and the world are often related to loss, danger and failure: 'People are always going to abandon me', 'The world is not a safe place', 'I am worthless'.

Although women who eventually seek coaching and other forms of professional assistance often have a long history of coping well and at a high level, it is important to understand the pattern of thinking and behaviour that may have led up to this point. If the decision problem is solved, but the underlying thoughts and behaviours that led to that stress reaction are not dealt with, she's likely to have more stress related problems that may manifest in other ways.

Whatever stage of the stress development path your coachee finds herself at, by using some of the exercises in this book, by listening intently to what she is actually saying and not filling in the gaps with what you *think* she is saying and by giving her the space to make up her own mind, you will give her everything she needs to feel confident once more about her decision making process. Use every ounce of your coaching genius to form an appropriate goal, to weave confidently in and out of the TGROW model and listen to make sure the coachee is heard, understood and acknowledged; then you will feel what it is like to coach a woman.

14 Qualifying as a Coach: Do You Need That Piece of Paper?

So now you've read our book and learned from our experience, are you ready to put a sign on your door saying 'qualified coach'? Well no, unless you've already qualified with us or with another ethical coaching trainer provider.

Of course, you will have learnt a lot by reading this book. You understand the key differences between coaching a woman and coaching a man. You've found out how to meet your female coachee's needs using the TGROW model and a number of other coaching exercises. But nothing can fully replace face-to-face learning and the ability to try out your new skills under the supervision and guidance of a qualified, experienced teacher who can help you to hone your skills and become really confident. So taking an accredited training course and gaining your qualification certificate is essential.

There are also practical reasons why you shouldn't either set up as a professional coach or coach within your organisation without that all important piece of paper. It would be madness to work as a coach without professional indemnity insurance, which you won't get without evidence of proper training and a qualification. It is rare for coaches to come up against someone who wants to take legal action against them but it can happen, as can accidents like tripping over a rug in your office. As well as protecting you financially against having to pay out damages, an insurance company will represent you and filter out any false claims. Another reason to have insurance is that if you want to hire a space in a professional venue they will probably ask for your insurance certificate, as will many public bodies and private businesses if they wish to hire you as a coach.

If you research available coaching courses you will find a bewildering number are on offer. How do you choose? We think that the following ingredients are those that matter most.

Is your training provider accredited with a reputable coaching organisation?

Although there isn't an overall official body to regulate the coaching industry, there are organisations such as the Association for Coaching (AC) and the International Coach Federation (ICF) which set standards for the industry. If they recognise a course then you can be reassured it will have come under intense scrutiny and will continue to be monitored for best practice.

Is the provider recognised or accredited with any other national non-coaching body?

For further reassurance find out if your chosen course has the backing of a non-coaching organisation. Organisations such as the National Open College Network (NOCN) and the Institute of Leadership and Management (ILM) also monitor coaching courses, ensuring that the content and the way it is taught come under rigorous investigation. Trainers must be able to demonstrate and show clear evidence, in various forms, to prove that their students have been well taught and that they comply with the conditions of their governing body.

How does the provider make sure that your work is assessed fairly?

Your provider should have in place:

1   An internal verification policy

2   An assessment policy

3   An assessment appeals procedure

4   Evidence of external verification of their assessments

These policies are there to make sure that you are completely clear about what you need to do in every aspect of the course, including how marks and grades are earned. The internal and external verifications are there to ensure that all your tutors are marking to the same standard. Someone outside their organisation will be monitoring the whole process on your behalf.

Do they offer a substantial amount of student contact with the tutors?

How much contact will you have before the course and while it is ongoing? Who is your contact? Even the most efficient and well meaning secretary or administrator won't have a real insight into the course and your training unless he or she has actually been on it, so make sure your tutors will be there for you.

Is most if not all of the course taught face to face rather than by distance learning?

We don't recommend any distance learning. No amount of DVDs are a substitute for a day's learning with your tutors and peer group.

How many face-to-face tuition hours will the course provide?

We recommend at least sixty – after all, you will be working with people on the things that matter most to them in the world. You don't want to let anyone down through lack of experience. Being able to ask questions as they arise and deal with any problems or fears when they occur will be extremely reassuring for a new coach.

How many hours of practice sessions should you expect to have to put in before you can qualify?

Sixty is our advice. Not only will you feel much more confident after so many hours of experience but you will also have had the opportunity to ask for testimonials or recommendations to put on your publicity material.

How big a group should you be looking for?

We recommend studying in small groups of ten to twelve. You will form strong links with other members of the group who will remain a support to you long after you've qualified. Also you will be more likely to get individual attention from your tutors in a group of ten than in a group of a hundred.

Does the provider behave ethically in not setting up false expectations in you?

We've come across coaching schools who give their prospective students the idea that they could soon be sitting on a beach somewhere earning fabulous money coaching coachees over the phone. While coaching is a very satisfying career, which can also be a high earner, we would like to see more attention paid to the realities of marketing yourself and building up a coachee base you can trust. Developing any business requires stamina and commitment.

Are the tutors practising coaches?

Why would you want to learn from anyone who wasn't putting into practice what they were teaching you? Your confidence will grow if you know that your tutors are using genuine examples to illustrate their teaching based on their own coaching coachees – real situations they've seen and actual case studies from those who have paid for coaching. Not only will this inspire you, but their experience will enhance your learning.

Although at present there is no overall body regulating coaching there are movements towards establishing industry standards. If you've trained with a reputable organisation they will be researching future possible industry standards and putting together their current courses with those standards in mind. They will be doing their utmost right now to ensure that your qualification will meet future standards.

How useful will your coaching skills be in life in general?

When choosing your coaching course provider, check out if the skills you will learn will be useful to you in other areas of your life, not just your work life. In other words, will you start to *live* the course material by using it to strengthen personal as well as professional relationships? Check this out by:

- Confirming if your chosen course encourages you to stay in contact with your fellow students between teaching sessions.

- Verifying if you will be taught skills which will be useful in relating to other people on a daily basis (e.g. listening skills).

- Asking your tutors how what you learn will help your own personal development and self knowledge.

Is the course a good fit for you?

Have a think about what your needs are and how the course will work around them:

- What provision is in place if you have to miss part of the training through ill health?
- What is the policy if you have a physical disability?
- How are complaints dealt with?

Your course provider should have in place:

1 An equal opportunities policy

2 A complaints procedure

3 A disability discrimination policy

These policies make sure that your course provider has thought about how to be fair to people with any special needs.

Is there an opportunity for you to be part of a community through your training organisation?

You might like to consider what provision your course provider has in place for you to continue to be a part of their professional community once you are qualified. You could ask what access you have to your tutors outside your set teaching hours and when the coaching course is over. Are there any opportunities to work with or write for your coaching provider to establish your career when you qualify? Also check how much time there is within the teaching schedule for discussion and feedback. All of these areas will be important once you start your course, so make sure you ask these questions before you commit.

Is there a real person on the end of a phone to answer your questions?

You might like to consider how much information you are given before you are expected to make a commitment to the course. Does the course provider object to you phoning to ask questions? Are you able to talk to someone (e.g. a past or current student) who has intimate knowledge of the course? Are the tutors available to talk you through your concerns?

How flexible is your course going to be?

Women have finally won the right to try out for any role they want. But there is a problem: the tasks just keep piling up. 'Women can't abandon one role to assume another ... multitasking has become a woman's survival response' (Popcorn and Marigold, 2000: 45). The chances are that whenever you decide to enrol on a coach training course you will have plenty more going on in your life. So:

- What will your training provider do if you fall behind with your work or miss deadlines?

- What flexibility is there if you unexpectedly find yourself in multitasking hell?

- What level of support and understanding can you expect?

All these questions will give you confidence as how to you will be treated and what expectations will be placed on you.

What background experience do your tutors have?

How does your course provider know what you will need in order to become a confident and competent expert in coaching? The chances are, if they've been there and done it, they will know without you even having to ask. Find out for your peace of mind:

- Are your tutors acknowledged experts with an established track record?

- Have your tutors published any relevant books or articles?

- Are your tutors 'working' coaches with their own professional practices?

- How long has your training provider been in business?

- What contact (if any) are you offered with past students?

- Do they have a code of ethics available?

- How much detail are you being given about the course?

What is your training provider doing to continue 'their' development forwards?

Every good training provider will be looking for ways to improve their service. If they ask you for feedback and give you the opportunity to comment, then you can be assured that they are constantly changing and working to be the best they can be.

We hope you've enjoyed the journey we have taken you on through this book and wish you good luck in choosing the right accredited course for you to be able to grow in a supportive and professional manner. Enjoy every minute of your new career … just as we do!

Bibliography

Alexander, Michele G. and Wendy Wood (2000). Women, men and positive emotions: a social role interpretation. In Agneta H. Fischer (ed.), *Gender and Emotion: Social Psychological Perspectives*. Cambridge University Press, pp. 189–210.

Archer, John and Barbara Lloyd (2002). *Sex and Gender* (2nd edn). Cambridge University Press.

Aspire Companies (2008). Women who make it work: the secrets of success for female leaders. Survey by Aspire Coaching and Leadership for senior women leaders. Available at www.aspirecompanies.com (accessed 10 May 2011).

Austen, Jane (2006/1817). *Persuasion*. Penguin.

Buskens, Ineke (2009). Doing research with women for the purpose of transformation. In Ineke Buskens and Anne Webb (eds), *African Women and ICTs: Investigating Technology – Gender and Empowerment*. Zed Books, pp. 9–18.

Carlson, Neil R. and William Buskist (1996). *Psychology: The Science of Behavior* (5th edn). Allyn & Bacon.

Cannon, Walter B. (1932) *The Wisdom of the Body*. Norton.

Chivers, Jessica (2011). *Mothers Work! How to Get a Grip on Guilt and Make a Smooth Return to Work*. Hay House.

Collins E. G. and P. Scott (1978). Everyone who makes it has a mentor. *Harvard Business Review* 56: 89–101.

Dorrance, Anson (2005). *The Vision of a Champion: Advice and Inspiration from the World's Most Successful Women's Soccer Coach*. Huron River Press.

Dorrance, Anson (n.d.). Coaching women: going against the instincts of my gender. Available at www.spartan.org/resources/coachingwomen.doc (accessed 10 May 2011).

Ecuyer-Dab, I. and M. Robert (2004). Have sex differences in spatial ability evolved from male competition for mating and female concern for survival? *Cognition* 91: 221–257.

Edwards, Gill (2007). *Life is a Gift*. Piatkus.

Fine, Cordelia (2011). *Delusions of Gender: The Real Science behind Sex Differences*. Icon.

Gilbert, Elizabeth (2010). *Committed*. Bloomsbury.

Glouberman, Dina (1989). *Life Choices and Life Changes through Image Work*. Unwin Paperbacks.

Goyder, Caroline (2009). *The Star Qualities*. Sidgwick & Jackson.

Gray, John (1992). *Men Are from Mars, Women Are from Venus*. HarperCollins.

Grossman, M. and W. Wood (1993). Sex differences in intensity of emotional experience: a social role interpretation. *Journal of Personality and Social Psychology* 65: 1010–1022.

Herring, S. C. (1994). Gender differences in computer-mediated communication: bringing familiar baggage to the new frontier. Keynote talk at panel entitled 'Making the Net*Work*: Is there a Z39.50 in gender communication?', American Library Association annual convention, Miami, 27 June 1994. Available at http://cpsr.org/prevsite/cpsr/gender/herring.txt/view (accessed 31 January 2012).

Jäncke, L. and H. Steinmetz (1994). Interhemispheric transfer time and corpus callosum size. *Neuroreport* 5: 2385–2388.

Kirschbaum, C., T. Klauer, S.-H. Filip and D.H. Hellhammer (1995). Sex-specific effects of social support on cortisol and subjective responses to acute psychological stress. *Psychosomatic Medicine* 57: 23–31.

Kline, Nancy (1999). *Time to Think*. Cassell Orion.

Kuebli, J., S. Butler and R. Fivush (1995). *Mother–Child Talk about Past Emotions: Relations of Maternal Language and Child Gender Over Time*. Cambridge University Press.

Leiberman, Simma (n.d.). Differences in male and female communication styles. Available at www.simmalieberman.com/articles/maleandfemale.html (accessed 10 May 2011).

McCall Smith, Alexander (2009). *Corduroy Mansions*. Polygon.

Moir, Anne and David Jessel (1998). *Brainsex: The Real Difference between Men and Women*. Arrow.

Nadeau, Robert L. (1996). *S/He Brain: Science, Sexual Politics and the Myths of Feminism*. Praeger.

Narain, Jaya (2010). Men are NOT from Mars and women are NOT from Venus: gender differences are 'down to how we are raised'. *Daily Mail*, 15 August. Available at www.dailymail.co.uk/news/article-1303270/Men-NOT-Mars-women-NOT-Venus--gender-differences-raised.html (accessed 10 May 2011).

Neenan, Michael and Windy Dryden (2002). *Life Coaching: A Cognitive Behavioural Approach*. Routledge.

Nejad, Lillian and Katerina Volny (2008). *Treating Stress and Anxiety: A Practitioner's Guide to Evidence-Based Approaches*. Crown House Publishing.

Pearson, Allison (2002). *I Don't Know How She Does It*. Chatto & Windus.

Pomerleau, A., D. Bolduc, G. Malcuit and L. Cossette (1990). Pink or blue: environmental gender stereotypes in the first two years of life. *Sex Roles* 22(5–6): 359–367.

Popcorn, Faith and Lys Marigold (2000). *EVEolution: The Eight Truths of Marketing to Women*. Hyperion

Quast, Lisa (2010). Forget the old quote 'Business is business, it's not personal'. Available at www.careerwomaninc.com/blog/?p=1108 (accessed 10 May 2011).

Robbins, Anthony (2001). *Notes from a Friend: A Quick and Simple Guide to Taking Charge of Your Life*. Pocket Books.

Sanders, L., Sander, P. and Mercer, J. (2009). Rogue males? Approaches to study and academic performance of male psychology students. *Psychology Teaching Review* 15(1): 3–17.

Shields, Stephanie A. (2000). Thinking about gender, thinking about theory: gender and emotional experience. In Agneta H. Fischer (ed.), *Gender and Emotion: Social Psychological Perspectives*. Cambridge University Press, pp. 3–23.

Shields, Stephanie A. (2002). *Speaking from the Heart: Gender and the Social Meaning of Emotion*. Cambridge University Press.

Tannen, Deborah (1995). *You Just Don't Understand: Women and Men in Conversation*. HarperCollins.

Taylor, S.E., L. C. Klein, B. P. Lewis, T. L. Gruenewald, R. A. R. Gurung and J. A. Updegraff (2000). Biobehavioral responses to stress in females: tend-and-befriend, not fight-or-flight. *Psychological Review* 107: 411–429.

Thomas, S. P. (1996). Women's anger: causes, manifestations, and correlates. In C. D. Spielberger, I. G. Sarason, J. M. T. Brebner, E. Greenglass, P. Laungani and O. M. O'Roark (eds), *Stress and Emotion: Anxiety, Anger, and Curiosity* (Vol. 15). Taylor & Francis, pp. 53–74.

Witelson, S. F., I. I. Glezer and D. L. Kigar (1995). Women have greater density of neurons in posterior temporal cortex. *Journal of Neuroscience* 15: 3418–3428.

Index

3

**For more information on qualifying
to become a coach, please visit**

www.ukcoachingpartnership.com

**For more information on *How to Coach a Woman*, join our
Facebook group and be part of the conversation**

www.facebook.com/How.to.Coach.a.Woman

Or to talk to us directly, call

0845 474 2251

CD-ROM Contents

- Coachee contact form
- Coachee feedback form
- Code of ethics and good practice
- Face-to-face coaching confirmation letter
- Goal setting using FEMALE and SMART
- Negative and positive circles
- Simple coachee terms and conditions
- Stress decision path
- Telephone confirmation letter
- The kind of values your coachee may think of
- The six key principles of coaching a woman
- The wheel of life and A values table
- Tips on blending TGROW with how a woman's mind works